DANGEROUS WEALTH

By Trish Jenkins

What Every Successful Woman Needs to Know to Avoid Being Ripped Off!

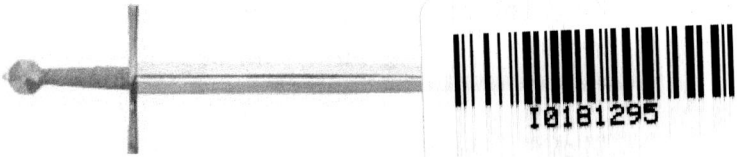

The Good, the Bad and the Ugly

A politically incorrect guide to avoiding (or bouncing back from) financial and romantic fraud.

Author: Trish Jenkins

Copyright © 2010 Patricia Jenkins

Title: *Dangerous Wealth: What Every Woman Needs To Know To Avoid Being Ripped Off!*

Edition: Second edition

Publisher: Trish Jenkins (Seasonz Pty. Ltd. Trading as Trish Jenkins)

ISBN: 978-0-646-52984-4

www.speakertrishjenkins.com

ENDORSEMENTS

"Trish Jenkins has written a practical and timely warning for all of us as women in business."

Liz Venzin
CEO Australia-Israel Chamber of Commerce 2003-2008

"Trish is very passionate about fraud prevention. Many women I deal with do not realize how easily they could have prevented a loss. Trish has written an easy to understand handbook that will help women protect their heart as well as their wealth."

Michael Featherstone
Chief Investigator, Phoenix Global
National Leader in Corporate and Private Investigation

"In her straight-talking, quirky style, Trish shares keys to avoiding rip-offs that will help women, men and churches to not only create but retain their blessing."

Mark Ramsey
International Speaker and Senior Pastor,
Citipointe Church, Brisbane, Australia

"Make no mistake; victims of crime are not random but selected by the predator! Trish has put together an insightful and powerfully empowering handbook that not only educates women on how to protect themselves from "human predators of the heart" as well as the pocket book; but also shows them how to draw on their own inner personal power to effectively take action!"

Earl Morris,
Co-Founder & Managing Director,
Lifeforce International and Protecting My Child, Inc., Gold Coast,
Australia

DEDICATION

This book is dedicated to the sons of Belial who

"have no faithfulness in their mouth;

Their inward part is destruction;

Their throat is an open grave;

They flatter with their tongue."

(Psalm 5:9)

Thank you for making me more successful in myself than I ever was when houses and money were my goals. I am determined to reduce the number of your victims and turn the tide on you.

I will train them.

I will equip them.

I am a Warrior Princess...

ACKNOWLEDGEMENTS

\\ **Justin.** My husband, my hero. When other men might have fled as they often do, you never shrank from defending and protecting me, even though it cost you everything you had. Adversity brought out your best and I fell in love with you all over again.

\\ **My little girls - Chelsea, Felicity and Olivia.** You are the reason I kept my sanity as the abyss threatened to pull me over its seductive edge.

\\ My faithful parents, all three of you, Ps Ian and Jan Ross and Peter Erwin.

\\ Ps Mark and Leigh Ramsey, for believing in me and never doubting I would turn my lemons into lemonade that serves others.

\\ Ps Jan Campbell, my friend and mentor of 20 years. You said, "Miracles are wonderful except when you need one!" You and Ps Clark Taylor remind me that I carry the Supernatural Power of God within me. When it was all I had, it was enough.

\\ Bob Harrison of www.increase.org, Os Hillman of www.marketplaceleaders.org, Tony Scown, Lyn Hamilton, Vicky Simpson (nee D'Orazio) and Tim Hall (It is well).

\\ My intercessors, Wesley, Jenny and Sandra www.businessblessings.com.au.

\\ My very wise editor, Jenny Wilson of www.originaltext.com.au.

\\ Photographers Linda Pasfield and John Olsen.

\ Lachlan McIntosh of KordaMentha, who audited every nook and cranny of my life! You taught me that it is always darkest before it goes completely black...but life still goes on.

\ The ASIC investigators, who opened my eyes to corporate justice as legally interpreted in my country. (How naïve I was).

\ My lawyers, who explained the relationship between resources and justice.

\ The many friends who lifted my arms at different times, you know who you are. Most of all to the One who makes a way where there is no way, the lifter of my head, all glory to You.

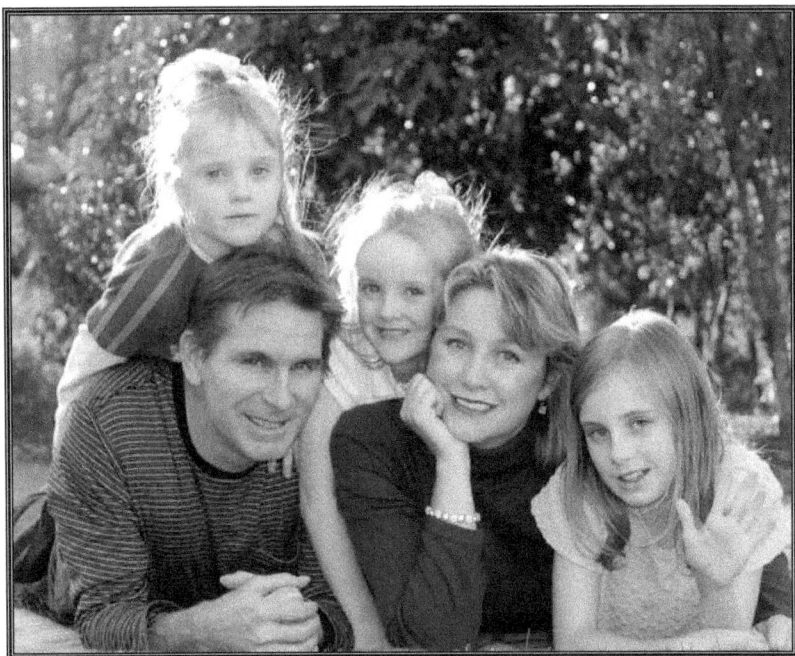

AUTHOR'S NOTE

Success is a double-edged sword. While it attracts opportunities, it also attracts opportunists.

I love prosperity books, but "how to's", passion, and even faith are not enough. To miss warning signals is to risk the loss of money, inner confidence and even relationships.

From 1998 to 2005 my husband and I invested so well that we achieved our "Dream". We no longer had to work and we were both still under 40!

However, over a few months it dissipated due to fraud with receivers and lawyers absorbing any leftovers. Before discovering I was being defrauded I tried to fix what I thought was a temporary problem my currency trader was having. In doing so, I breached the Corporations Act.

I served 8 months imprisonment for my breach. I had not stolen any money, but I had caved under pressure and made a wrong decision, bad enough for a term of incarceration.

A story worth telling, but not in this book; visit my website: www.speakertrishjenkins.com for "Treasures of Darkness: A Prison Journey" detailing my personal prison experiences and lessons learned.

Well, what doesn't kill you makes you stronger...or at least gives you a great story to tell. I do not write this book as a sob story. I write this book as a warning to the unwary, an encouragement to those already burned and a testimony to the grace of God who can turn any ugly situation into something worthwhile, if we let Him.

This is not a religious book, although spiritual people, including Christians, will find answers in these pages; especially if fraud has damaged your faith.

You can suffer and self-destruct with grief, resentment and anger after a betrayal; or you can make the dirt into a pile that enables you to stand taller and gives you a better view.

The first thing you will see from the top of your dirt pile is that truth can hurt. It was painful enough to face the truth about myself, but what I learned about others was equally painful.

Silly, I know, but I had forgotten the old saying, "Everyone is your friend when you are making money". You do find out who your real friends are in a crisis. Sometimes the revelation is surprising! I have found out the hard way that the betrayal of fraud is only slightly more painful than the judgment of "fair-weather" friends.

Ironically, the successful friends I looked up to before are still my friends. They understood more than anyone else did. They cared enough to give me advice as I climbed back up.

If you have suffered from financial or romantic fraud, you are not alone and you can heal. I invite you to renew your faith and strength in these pages.

If you are successfully slaying your giants, I offer you tools to protect your rearguard and enhance your vision.

"Most of us are like the rest of us." We would all like financial security and freedom. We all have a need to be loved. We all want to be able to trust those with whom we deal.

Fraud has causes. It has effects. If we put aside our sensitivities and politically correct conditioning, we can protect ourselves from the villains among us...and from ourselves.

There is light at the end of the tunnel that may not be an oncoming train...Just be sure you can tell the difference!

Put your slippers on and grab a "cuppa". Come over to your favorite reading spot. Have a highlighter pen or a pad and pencil handy on the side table if you are inclined to make notes.

Let's begin.

Trish

Note: I have changed many of the names and details of situations in this book to protect the innocent, the guilty and the stupid...

This message is for an international audience because fraud knows no boundaries. Please refer to your own state or country's regulatory bodies that would be relevant to your particular situation.

Contents

PART 3: MOVING FORWARD............143

PART 1:

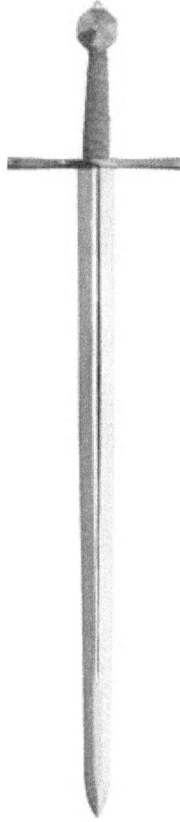

UNCOMFORTABLE TRUTHS

Chapter One

The Warrior Princess...

...And Her Sword

The double-edged sword is a metaphor for wealth. It can achieve both great and terrible things.

You, dear reader, are a warrior with a sword in your hand. The size and quality matter not. How well you wield it will depend on you. You are responsible for the care and use of your sword. However:

It is not the sword that creates the power.

It is the wielder of the sword...

You.

You are amazing.

The Nitti-Gritty

Wealth creation is fantastic. It is rewarding, fun and can really make a difference beyond your own life. Whether your passion is to feather your own nest, or build orphanages, the process is the same.

1. You find an opportunity.

2. You invest in the opportunity.

3. The opportunity provides a yield.

However, like the chapter headings of a book, there is always more to it than that! What is the point of making wealth if someone sees you as his or her opportunity, and takes it from you? You can have all the asset protection money can buy but that will not help if you trust the wrong person.

It is much more efficient to learn from someone else's mistakes than from our own.

I love the quote by Catherine Aird, "If you can't be a good example, then you'll just have to be a horrible warning!" I never thought I would serve as the latter.

My intention is not to scare you but rather, help you become more skillful so that your life can hold and manage greater abundance. If something in this book prevents a loss in your life, you will have made a fortune, (after all a dollar saved is better than a dollar earned).

Today my life is a "testimony to turnaround". I have been humbled yet empowered. Success really is about perspective. From the mountaintops of success to the deep valleys of despair and loss, the lessons I have learned are priceless. I have contentment and joy in my life that is not money based. I have rebuilt my life and I look forward to the future.

No one can take away the skills and knowledge you have accumulated. Every warrior takes a hit now and then. Borrow from my strength until you find your own. You will rise up again. I choose not to be a victim and neither should you.

Reading the Play

Spotting fraud is a lot like reading body language. Any one signal can be innocent. Deception usually becomes apparent when there is a cluster of signals.

Even then, if you do not know what to look for, you can be like many creditors who continue to believe empty promises because the bleedingly obvious truth is unacceptable.

Unreturned calls are rude but may not mean fraud. The person may just be disorganized or too busy. (BTW: "too busy" means your business is not important enough to them.) Either way, business with such a person is risky.

Wealth is only one level of success. Maturity is being able to recover from setbacks and be able to protect your future success. This book will help you do that. Inside every woman are both a Warrior and a Princess. Sometimes it takes great adversity to discover them.

 *The choice between Victim and Warrior Princess is ours.*

Between Christmas 1998 and 2005, my husband and I accumulated enough properties and cash flow producing investments to the point that we no longer needed to work. We simply managed our investments, distributed funds to our chosen charities and looked for more opportunities. It was a very exciting time.

Great leaders and wealth creation "gurus" inspired us.

In 2002, "Rich Dad, Poor Dad" author and guru, Robert Kiyosaki interviewed us on television about our journey. Others wanted to do what we had done as it looked like we were "Living the Dream!"

Above: Justin, Me, Kym and Robert Kiyosaki

During that heady period we were blessed with our 3 daughters, so I was also popular with women who would ask, "How on earth have you found the time?"

"I figured if I'm going to have a hobby, it should be one that benefits my family, not just me!" was my practical answer.

People came from afar taking us to lunch or coffee in order to pick our brains. Our response was always that we do not give personal financial advice. We did recommend reading:

1. Rich Dad Poor Dad : Robert Kiyosaki and Sharon Lechter

2. Who Moved My Cheese? : Dr Spencer Johnson

3. The Richest Man in Babylon : George S. Clason

4. The Prayer of Jabez : Bruce Wilkinson

5. The Storehouse Principle : Al Jandl and Van Crouch

When they returned, I would encourage them to read more books and be givers.

Being generous makes a way for blessings. However, I also encouraged people to give, because it would expose any greed in their hearts that would hamper them from doing business in a win-win kind of way.

Then my "cheese" was moved...!

Some people we invested with turned out to be frauds.

My currency trader had persuaded me to be a "contact" person for his investors so he could concentrate on his trading. He also set up a registered managed fund approved by the ASIC (Australian Securities and Investments Commission) based on his trading. Looking back, the warning signals were there, but I did not see them, as I did not then know what they might be.

Clearly neither did the ASIC.

This trader was a clever liar and a fraud. My own family, friends, and people I did not even know personally lost millions of dollars.

In the same year, our financial advisor, also our accountant went into liquidation along with several hundred thousand dollars we had invested with him. Many of the same friends had also invested with him.

The legal issues were traumatic and expensive. Not knowing I was being deceived, I tried to temporarily fix an impossible situation. As a result I breached the Corporations Act. Our company went into liquidation and we went back to work in order to live and keep lawyers well fed.

Although devastated by the losses, I was more horrified that I played a role in other people losing money.

There was nowhere to hide my shame.

While most of my friends insisted that no one had twisted their arms and they were responsible for their own investment decisions, there were those who thought I should have known better or even suspected I had stolen their money.

Fortunately, the independent audit that followed showed I had not. However, I had still broken the law and was charged with fraud.

The entire legal process took years and culminated in 8 months of incarceration for breaching the Corporations Act. The lead prosecutor later told me she had expected me to go home instead.

I was angry but I thought philosophically, "Criminals do what criminals do". Ironically, the nasty reactions of a few people hurt me more than the betrayal of the fraudster.

 It was strangely easy to forgive and not feel deep animosity toward someone who had played me like a Stradivarius.

 Money and betrayal affect people in the deepest way.

At the time, it was harder to forgive a few friends turning on me; those who I thought "knew" me. People lash out when they are hurt and angry, I cannot judge them for that.

I knew I was entering a dark valley. I could not afford the extra baggage of unforgiveness weighing me down. I was going to learn a lot more about that over the next few years.

Forgiveness is not easy when you are hurt and misunderstood. Hurting people can be the most hurtful people. Negative energy will only sustain you until you burn out. Inner freedom creates peace, hope, and even joy.

None of that comes from money:

But we have this treasure in jars of clay to show that this all-surpassing power is from God and not from us. We are:

- hard pressed on every side, but not crushed;

- perplexed, but not in despair;

- persecuted, but not abandoned;

- struck down, but not destroyed.

2 Corinthians 4:7-9

In regards to "flocks", spiritual people are particularly vulnerable to fraud because they often believe an opportunity is a blessing from the Lord or the "Universe".

"Walking by faith, not by sight" does not mean being naïve. Jesus calls us to be "wise as a serpent but gentle as a dove". (Matthew 10:16)

The Bible has excellent advice and cautions when it comes to business. However, like children suffering from "selective hearing," people can often suffer from scriptural "selective reading".

Leaders are not immune to the handicap either.

So if you are a person of faith, honor your leaders but realize they are only human.

This goes for devotees of motivational or otherwise spiritual leaders too!

Pedestals are for statues not people.

Truth hurts but ignorance has consequences that are more painful. The good news is that every negative experience contains in it a lesson of value. While I would prefer to have not lost everything, I am a stronger, smarter and more compassionate person because of it.

I learned how to overcome an adversity that would cripple most Westerners. Let us not kid ourselves: Money can be just as much a pagan idol as a carved statue of the East. To be truly financially free the Warrior Princess needs to know how to be content in good times and bad. That attitude opens the door to true prosperity. To achieve this, she needs to know herself and her true worth.

Like the Proverbs 31 woman, I can now smile at the future... and you can too.

Identity

"What's your name?

What's your father?!!"

The shrill voices of upper class school girls "blood" the new kid in Henry Handel Richardson's classic, "The Getting of Wisdom". This was the first attempt to pigeonhole young Laura Rambotham in the private school pecking order.

A person's family connections, school and profession once defined their success. While "the old school tie" may provide introductions, it will not guarantee success. In the modern world, many traditional occupations have become obsolete.

I remember when the smartest people in the class would go on to study medicine or law. Then the smart kids realized that I.T. was the way to go to make the big bucks.

After a while, as is the way of supply and demand, I.T. guys became a dime a dozen, technology became simpler. Suddenly, they were no longer able to command the money they once could.

If our identity is what we do, we will wind up with multiple personality disorder. Perhaps this contributes to the reports of increased stress and the feeling of not being "connected" with society. We are without a feeling of destiny, without a sense of our "place" in the world.

We continue playing on the playground of life, going from the slide to the swing to the roundabout until dusk. In real life, we call it "Busyness" and "stuff" collection.

The need to collect STUFF will make you a target for fraud. A later chapter will address how to recognize if you are a target, and how to remedy that situation.

It has been said that multi-millionaires have had an average of seven different businesses over their journey. Some businesses they grew and sold off, others went "bust". Their ability to bounce back was not based on their identity as a car salesperson, a lawyer or an MLM distributor.

It was their confidence in who they were and their ability to regroup and go again.

 Being too BUSY can make you VULNERABLE to fraud.

First Fraud Exposed:

It does not matter how impressive or otherwise your occupation is, what every successful person needs to expose and settle in their heart, is the following:

1. You are not what you do.

2. Your value does not come from your wealth.

Unless you accept these truths, recovering from financial or romantic fraud will be very difficult.

Lessons learned:

✓ You can never tell how normal people will react when their money is under threat!

✓ You can only repent of your own sin; you cannot carry the guilt of other people's decisions.

Recently I attended my 20-year school reunion at Toorak College in Mt. Eliza, Victoria. It could have been the film location for "The Getting of Wisdom" mentioned earlier.

I had planned to sweep in on waves of success, impressing them all with my business acumen.

I had become a multi-millionaire by being very clever. I had not inherited it and I had not married it. I was proud.

My schoolmates would beg to be a part of my ventures. However, by the time said reunion came around; I was in the midst of an ugly fraud investigation. My reputation was under a cloud. So much had gone wrong; I had even lost our family home.

During the trip I caught up with a childhood friend, now a lawyer married to an obstetrician, (something I now cynically thought I should have done.)

It was hard to enjoy the trendy setting of Melbourne's internationally renowned Lygon Street. The excellent Italian cuisine could have been cardboard to my depressed taste buds.

I got advice from one about the state of my finances and advice from the other about the state of my pelvic floor muscles (the result of twins) as both areas were unreliable.

My sensible friend and her kind husband gave me their best observation from years in both practices:

> "The only thing people care about more than their health
>
> ... is their money!"

12

Bounce Back

Bouncing back is not only possible, it is obligatory. Without healing, a person can become embittered and fearful of trying again.

Well, not only have my pelvic floors recovered, I have since learned skills to invest smarter. When you have the right weapons and the skill to use them, you will be a victim no longer. You will be a Warrior Princess.

 Human beings deserve dignity and respect.

We women are complex beings. We have a variety of roles and we play them with varying degrees of skill. We are mothers, wives, girlfriends, daughters, sisters, friends, bosses, employees, entrepreneurs etc. Apart from these roles, we can have issues with our personal value. Sometimes we mistakenly measure our value by how well we meet the needs of those whose role dictates our own.

A Radical Idea

I would like to suggest a controversial idea so radical that it flies in the face of our modern goal-setting, climb-the-ladder, politically correct, self-actualizing, New-Age, antidepressant swallowing, busy, busy, busy, society.

Are you ready for this?

You are NOT a highly evolved piece of goop.

Nor are you a deity trying to get her act together!

Really, don't you think a "goddess" would have a handle on things a smidge better than we do?

Your value does not come from your career, your business turnover, (or turnovers between the sheets). Nor does it come from what your family said about you.

You are valuable simply because
you are a human being.

You are a marvelous creation designed with a purpose. A sense of purpose is essential for the successful woman. Is it any wonder Rick Warren's Purpose Driven Life is a runaway best-seller?

A life lived on purpose is less likely to be distracted by "questionable" opportunities.

Your business and your wealth are tools you use for creating your destiny. When you know who you are and what you are truly worth, you are less likely to fall victim to fraud.

1. **Fraud of the heart**

2. **Fraud of the finance**

You may not achieve great things in the eyes of the world, but good things are great and noble when they are a sincere part of who you are. They will naturally reflect your calling.

You are a daughter of the Most High, the Creator of the Universe - The King of kings.

That makes you a Princess, not just any princess...

A "WARRIOR" PRINCESS

Absolute Value

Being taken advantage of does not decrease your intrinsic value. It only affects the value of the transient things in your life. Unfortunately, many people believe that without their wealth, they have no value. Being clever does not make you more valuable than someone who is clueless.

Repeatedly making foolish decisions does not diminish your intrinsic value; it simply means that you do not recognize your value sufficiently to protect yourself by seeking wisdom and strategies that will protect your vulnerability.

A company may place a monetary value on your skills, but that does not make you a more valuable person than someone who is a skilled homemaker or indeed, someone without any skills. Our world is about performance.

My 5th grade teacher had us regularly play a game called "Values Clarification". We would each play a character arguing for a place in a lifeboat. It was supposedly designed to help us improve our communication skills.

The problem is that impressionable minds were being trained to value those who were useful to us and to devalue, to actually discard, those who were not.

The worst part was being encouraged to say why someone else should not be included. It was very much a forerunner of the popular TV program "Survivor" today.

Of course, those values had a way of sticking with the child even in the playground long after the "game" was over.

> Society respects and values those
> who make money, because money has
> become society's priority.

Is it any wonder our society has not valued and respected those who are unable to add monetary value to society?

These are not just the poor, the mentally ill, the elderly, the sick, the handicapped or the stay-at-home mums.

In business, they are the "back office" of a corporation. These people need to justify the value of their contribution, unlike the sales department that simply points to sales figures.

A sales team can only function well if the back office is functioning well. It is a larger team at play.

In the same way, ordinary mums and dads are investing in the future workforce of our country.

Parents are the undervalued Human Resource Managers of the nation.

Further, training our children to care for and respect those who cannot care for themselves will be an investment into their character.

This too will have a flow on effect on the workforce they enter as adults. Such people are the strength of a company.

The monetary value of your skills will fluctuate with the ebb and flow of the marketplace.

Your intrinsic value is inestimable and unchangeable.

Princess,

Pick up your sword.

Take The Princess Warrior Challenge...

- Ask yourself these questions:
- Do I believe I am worthy of love and respect?
- If I were not able to do what I do now to create an income, would I still be important?
- To whom?
- Am I of greater or lesser value than a poverty stricken teenager in Cambodia?
- Why or why not?
- Am I convinced of my value?
- Where does my current sense of value come from?
- Do I feel like it changes with my performance or with my mood?
- How can I find an objective, constant, absolute value of myself?
- Do I know my purpose in this life?

Chapter Two

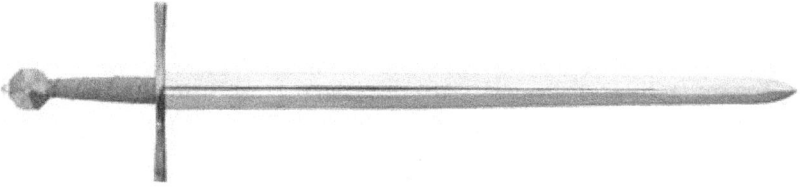

Types of Scams...

Romantic and Business

"That which has been is what will be, that which is done is what will be done, and there is nothing new under the sun."

Ecclesiastes 1:9

The prevalence of dishonesty in society can be traced back to The Garden of Eden when the serpent deceived Eve into disobeying the one rule in the garden.

Today, all frauds are simply old frauds dressed up in a new frock. The problem is that a new generation arises not knowing that what looks new, is really second hand.

> "Those who cannot remember the past are condemned to repeat it."

George Santayana

Each generation will be as gullible as its predecessors unless they allow history to teach them otherwise. Business degrees may provide units on Corporate Governance and the Legal Environment, but that does not necessarily equip a business graduate against deception.

Unfortunately, that qualification is usually taught at the "School of Hard Knocks" followed by the "University of Adversity"! Fraud can be as simple as a big brother cheating his little brother by swapping a $1 coin for the smaller $2 coin, or a dime for the smaller quarter. After all, until the little brother learns the meaning of monetary value, size is what counts.

We are not much different. Someone once said "If you are going to tell a lie, tell a whopper!" After all "truth is often stranger than fiction", and so the clichés go on. They are what enable us to believe what we want to, in spite of the warnings to the contrary.

Often an opportunity is so good that it becomes a carrot dangled in front of our desirous eyes. A normal business deal should be dealt with coolly. Risks and benefits must be carefully weighed.

According to Mr. Jody Elliss, best-selling author, futures trader and one of my most respected finance mentors, the number one rule of trading is:

NEVER RISK MORE THAN YOU CAN AFFORD TO LOSE!

Number 2 rule is: SEE RULE NUMBER 1!

A scam is designed to be so appealing that our ability to weigh its credibility is compromised.

Scam #1: Bait and Switch

This scam is one in which the advertised product is switched for an inferior one. It may be the quality of the engine in a car; something you may not check out until the service is due.

It could be an advertised property at an unbelievable price that was never really available for sale. It is used to "get the phone ringing" so you can be sold another one. Perhaps you have made a purchase online and the product has either not arrived or not been exactly what you ordered.

Shopping online can be dangerous if the seller is unknown. Most online auction sites such as eBay provide a facility where you can check out the seller's reputation from a buyer feedback section. Always use a secure site when entering your personal details. It is usually symbolized by a padlock in the bottom corner of the screen.

Scam #2: Product and Service Claims

- False and misleading health claims on products are prevalent. Many children's breakfast foods claim to be healthy because they are low in fat but can be extremely high in sugar or salt.

- Weight loss program scams.

- Affinity fraud: Nearly half of all investment frauds target members of a religious, ethnic or community group.

- Home repair rip-offs and pre-sale homes: The contracting industry is plagued by fraudsters. It's important to get quotes from more than one accredited contractor before agreeing to have any work done.

- License numbers: Whether it is for a tradesman or an "off-shore" bank; contact the relevant body to verify a license number. Anyone can have a series of numbers printed on a business card.

- Carbon credit and environment friendly claims on products.

- Diluted products: A pest inspection company was prosecuted for spraying concrete foundations with water instead of the pest barrier, leaving the property completely unprotected.

We should not assume one claim infers another benefit to us. As mentioned, something claiming to be 'low in sugar' is not automatically healthy.

Scam #3: Internet Fraud Identity theft

Thieves can steal your personal information from almost anywhere.

Phishing and Vishing

Even though the internet is relatively new, requests for the use of a person's bank account through which to funnel a dead person's estate, is not a new trick. An email might ask you to go to a particular site to confirm your details which are then stolen.

Vishing is the same scam over the phone. You are asked to call a given number for your financial institution. When you call the number there is a voice recording that prompts you to press buttons that correspond to your account. The result is the same. Your identity is stolen.

Some thieves will create an identical website to that of a reputable company, so always verify its authenticity by calling that company directly.

Checking checks/cheques

A common scam is when a "buyer" sends a check for more money than is actually required and asks you to return their "change". The best thing to do is give it to the authorities.

Even if someone pays for goods by check, do not send the goods until the check has been cleared in your account.

Scam #4: Internet Romance

Internet romance is a minefield. Kim, an attractive doctor in her 40s, had little time to date. She registered with an online dating service and began corresponding with Oliver, a computer programmer with a German bank.

Kim believed they had chemistry.

Oliver always seemed to understand how she was feeling and she could always tell when he was feeling "down".

They seemed to click. He was to come out and join her but there was a hold up with his accounts due to his ex-wife being "difficult".

He reluctantly revealed that he was still sorting out the financial arrangements after his divorce. Because he was so successful, his wife was really being difficult by trying to clean him out.

His assets were tied up due to court procedures. (Warning signal!)

Eventually, after much concerned prodding by Kim, he said that if he was just able to pay his wife 10,000 pounds, he could settle things and be free. However, he couldn't pay it until his assets were untied and they would not be untied until he paid it.

Oh, what was he to do?

Kim decided to help him out so that he could join her and repay the money once he could access his funds.

He was playing her of course. Kim believed that if she gave him the money he would be able to come out to Australia to join her.

She wired Oliver the money and some more money for his fare out. However, there were "delays", you know how the legal system is, it just drags on, just a few papers to sign, oh dear, they went to the wrong address...etc. etc.

Eight months later he was still not coming out and she has not been paid back. Legal issues do take time and are a very handy excuse for people not repaying money.

A year later, Kim is still waiting and hoping.

Occasionally she gets firm with her online lover but he is so sweet she feels guilty for doubting him.

The sad fact is that if matters are continually held up, you might as well accept there will not be any money forthcoming. You should move on with your life. Wishful thinking will not make it appear.

If it does come back, well it's a bonus, but it's more likely that any money that is freed up will be paid to lawyers and not you.

Personal Safety:

If you do meet someone on the internet, do not give out your address. If you want to meet, do so in a public place and make sure you tell at least two friends where you will be and for how long. Ask one of them to call you at some time during the "date" just to make sure you are all right and give you a polite excuse to leave. Better still, ask your friends to be at another table in the same place to keep an eye on you. If anything were to happen at a later date, they will be able to provide a description of the person.

Chapter Three

Why???

Understanding the Enemy

"We have met the enemy... and he is us."

Walt Kelly

Fraud is the use of deception to mislead a victim into believing something that is not true, for unlawful gain or unjust advantage.

This chapter will look at two kinds of wrong-doing. There is the person who tells lies of convenience or opportunity; and in a whole other league, is the con-artist.

Con-artists believe that what they do is simply their business. If a person believes them, it is their own fault.

The other kind is the dishonesty that comes from falling into temptation, or trying to use one mistake to fix another. I contacted a leading university (that shall remain nameless) to ask about the teaching of ethics in business. After all, fraud is the majority of "white-collar" crime.

To my dismay, in a business degree I found just one unit that was combined with a unit on business law.

 Ethics are not about the law. They are about doing what is right, not finding a legal way to be dishonest.

Good character is doing what is right when nobody is looking.

I'm not convinced that knowing the law and valuing "Ethics" is the same thing.

In great distress, a tradesman, David, called me about a statement the authorities wanted him to sign in regard to fraud charges they were trying to lay against a fellow scam victim, who happened to be his friend.

His friend, Peter, a builder, had not realized his role in a chain of supply, was unlawful at the time. Peter thought he was helping the authorities make things right.

The real scammer higher up the chain was in hiding, so the authorities were concentrating on the "little fish". The process of statement taking may vary from place to place, but in this instance it all appeared very innocent.

1. Lawyers took notes of what David told them, then went away to turn them into a formal statement for him to check and sign off.

2. David noticed several wrong points in the statement, corrected them and waited for them to return with a corrected draft.

3. What they returned had been changed even further with additional points that they did not point out to him.

4. David thought this odd, but the two lady lawyers were very nice and said it was no bother to fix it up again.

5. He fixed it and they returned again. This time the changes were even worse with complete fabrications added in.

6. David began to suspect they were hoping he would not want to be bothered anymore and just sign off on it.

7. He stood his ground regarding the account and the lawyers did not return to finish the statement.

David was convinced they were more interested in creating a damning statement against his friend, Peter than recording the truth.

> We can have so much confidence in ourselves that we think we are a better judge of character than we really are.

Sadly, my research has found others have not noticed that certain language has been inserted into their statements. This may appear to make little difference to the content, except that in legal terms, definitions of words can change and give a different meaning to what is being alleged.

Is the practice legal? Yes.

Is it ethical?

For some that depends on who the particular lawyer is working for...the ones in the preceding story were working for the government. Not a corrupt, third-world government, but the government of a "leading nation".

Be warned, bad things do happen to good people.

Well-intentioned friends do get into trouble after unwittingly becoming embroiled in an investment scheme. Our pride in our success (due, of course, to our brilliance) can make us overlook the need for thorough due-diligence.

> A healthy self-esteem can create a blind-spot.

"Department of Justice [U.S.] studies show that people with some college training or a college degree, are the most susceptible to con-artist scams." From CUFF, a 501 (c) (3) Non-Profit Corporation that Works to Bring Justice to Fraud Victims and Tracks Fugitives Who Evade Justice.

Crooks, con-artists and compromisers are all around us. They are people who look like us.

The scammers have practiced their handshaking skills; in fact they can pick your pocket at the same time!

The days of "judging a man by the firmness of his handshake", are over.

A Wrong Assumption

When I began to study how con-artists think, I thought I already had a fair idea. I had assumed it was our modern, relativistic society that created con-artists or fraudsters. I expected that, like criminals, a high percentage would come from families who were "dysfunctional". I imagined that they were brought up in a home where values were relative. That is, perhaps they were taught by example that lying is okay for the sake of convenience.

For instance, a child answers the phone and the parent says, "Tell them I'm not here."

Simple, regular dishonesty creates a value system that makes lying seem okay.

There are also the parents who teach children that there really is no right and wrong...as long as you are not hurting anyone. Perhaps this is an adulterous father, or alcoholic mother.

It might even be a relative who is sexually abusing a child. Pedophiles often claim they do not believe that they are doing any harm.

When children or young people have been betrayed and abused, they may decide that no-one can be trusted and that it's a "dog-eat-dog world, so only look out for No.1". This has been a popular business philosophy during the 20th century.

My wrong assumption went even further. At the very least, I expected that if dishonest people came from middle class "respectable" families, then there was an explanation for their behavior.

They may have been spoiled or were part of an emotionally weak family and therefore couldn't take correction or practice self-control because the adults couldn't. This would breed someone who was easily offended and not able to take responsibility for their own failures, allowing them to justify bad behavior.

 Being dishonest does not make a person a sociopathic con-artist.

Such values can affect the character of a person and influence how they treat business associates and their life partners, possibly making them a skilled manipulator and liar.

When problems are always the fault of someone else, a child will learn that even his or her own dishonesty is enabled because someone else provided an opportunity. Then it's a short step to actually blaming the victim.

However, such an environment will not necessarily make someone a con-artist; it will just make them weak in character.

Such people are in fact, more likely to be a target of a con, because they never learn from their mistakes. They believe their mistakes are always the fault of someone else!

My thinking was corrected the more I looked into what creates a con-artist. One thing I discovered was that a con-artist makes a career from deceit.

I was also mistaken in my assumptions about the history of the professional con-artist. I now know that the term "con" comes from the word "confidence". A con-artist wins a person's "confidence". We are more likely to trust those who present like ourselves.

> Only when he has won their trust, will the confidence trickster be able to relieve the victim of their money or of something else they value.

All Backgrounds

My research came from finance professionals, lawyers, victims who do not wish to be named, from books and websites such as straightshooter.net and of course my own horrendous 5-year experience.

I am particularly indebted to professional investigator Michael Featherstone of Phoenix Global for allowing me to become part of his company for 6 months to draw from his lifetime of experience in catching fraudsters.

Con-artists come from any and every kind of background, whether it is liberal or conservative, intellectual or sporting, dysfunctional or traditional, any religion, rich or poor, regardless of race or appearance. They have no conscience about what they do.

> Con-artists are highly intelligent, master manipulators.

Manipulation is a skill developed from a very young age. Instead of being sorry for being caught and learning a positive lesson from that; the lesson they learn is how to get away with it next time.

They learn there are short cuts to getting what they want. There is a thrill to the game for a child and the game continues when they reach adulthood.

The habit of taking shortcuts to fortune is what attracts so many con-artists to the financial seminar circuit. (That is not to say that the speaking circuit is full of con-artists. There are many excellent wealth creation speakers.)

Often con-artists enjoy role-playing, secretly casting others as characters in their play, which are totally unaware that they are now acting in a nasty game...

A recent con in the US was a 20-year-old Virginia woman going door-to-door posing as a cheerleader fund-raising for the local high school. She looked like a normal, sweet young lady, yet it turned out she had a history of fundraising deception.

I met an adorable aboriginal woman who looked about 14. I'll call her "Annie". Annie told me how she used to knock on the doors of lovely homes. When the usually white, well-off homeowners answered, they were confronted by a waif with big brown eyes and a hopeful expression. Annie would claim to have been adopted as a baby and that this was the last known address of her real family...can they help her? (Australia has a controversial history chapter regarding the adoption of Aboriginal children. It is referred to as "The Stolen Generation" so it's a tender subject.)

Annie would then keep the, by now, tearful homeowners occupied while her boyfriend slipped in the back to burgle the house! I was stunned as she explained, "It's more of an adrenalin rush when they are home!" Annie grinned mischievously as she assured me it wouldn't happen anymore because she is off drugs... I just hope she isn't an "adrenalin junkie!"

In the early 20th century, studies were done to look for a genetic reason for criminal behavior. Criminals were studied and their features logged.

These studies provided dubious justification for the practice in 1930s' Germany, of measuring noses to identify Jews. The Nazi regime connected aberrant behavior with race and appearance. However, the studies turned out to be inconclusive.

There was no proof that certain physical features inclined a person towards criminal behavior.

The media of the 20th century was fascinated by this concept as it made characters very entertaining. Movies and cartoons began to educate society with stereotypes of who the good guy is: The handsome Anglo; and who the bad guy is: The cowboy with the heavy moustache and the black hat.

> There is a mix of good and bad in all groups; we know this but we are still influenced by media stereotypes.

Ironically, the 21st century has seen a rise of media stereotyping; that is anyone representing "traditional" values are hypocritical deceivers. I love the show "Law and Order" but rarely have I seen an episode where a minister is not portrayed as corrupt.

A wonderful exception is the third Spiderman movie where Peter Parker explores his dark side. In the end it's about choosing which way we will go. The media definitely plays a role in influencing our trust through stereotyping characters.

> A racial appearance does not indicate untrustworthiness.

Nor should we be so "politically correct" that we ignore disturbing signals in a person's appearance that could reveal something about their personality and character.

Reading signals can also help indicate whether a person is likely to fit into the corporate culture of your firm. If your clients are risk-averse and elderly, a young person with safety pins through his eyebrows and tattoos of devils and naked women up his arms will have to work harder to win their confidence.

It would also be prudent to find out what the motivation was behind such an appearance.

According to Earl Morris, Protective Security Advisor, the 80s and early 90s were a time when politically correct American culture said, "It doesn't matter what I do in my spare time. My job is separate and my personal life has no bearing on my work life."

History has found this to be unrealistic. Earl specializes in risk management, including handling potentially violent situations in the workplace. Nine times out of ten, physical threats in the workplace had their roots in upsets in a person's personal life. Stalkers can harass a person at work, drug addiction does not stop when a person "clocks on".

> A clean cut appearance does not indicate trustworthiness.

While appearances are deceiving, I would not go so far as to say we should never judge a book by its cover. After all, the purpose of a book cover is to reflect its contents even though some can be misleading.

However, a person who goes to lengths to look like a "baddie" should not be surprised if he is treated with caution. Generally they have their own reasons to appear intimidating.

Sure, it could be a cry for help, but a woman is taking a great risk by entrusting her life and her children to someone like that. Just remember, if you have experienced hurt, betrayal or abuse in the past, then most likely your heart has a "faulty radar" when it comes to good judgment and discernment.

> You will seldom "spot" a dishonest person. A professional con-artist does not look like a "baddie".

Expert fraud investigator, Michael Featherstone of Phoenix Global, states: "One man with a briefcase can steal more money than ten men with guns".

Three things you can be sure of:

✓ There are dishonest people.

✓ There are con-artists.

✓ There are people who will be dishonest when put under pressure.

Before you start to feel superior, I suggest you think back to the last time your friend asked if her bottom looked big in that ridiculous dress…and your answer was…?

While the consequences of dishonesty vary, the focus of this book is financial and romantic fraud.

A con-artist will generally listen to you while you reveal your politics, your faith, what you consider important and most of all, what you need. They will then present themselves, chameleon-like as someone who fits in with those values.

I thought I saw an opportunity to make a difference in the world by sowing my investment returns into causes I believed in.

My hot button was philanthropy; fueled by my faith. While I did not expect the person I invested with to be a Christian, he talked about his Catholic upbringing; being a generous person by nature; citing impressive examples such as giving his car away; and New Age-like faith in the Universe to bring Karma-like rewards to his generosity.

Given the recent popularity of faith in a benevolent Universe, I didn't find this philosophy unusual.

 Not all dishonest behavior is illegal.

Sometimes, a person is robbed of their innocence. The betrayal of the heart can be more devastating than an actual robbery. Things can be replaced; virginity cannot. Whatever your views on the value of virginity, no-one has the right to take it through trickery, deception or force.

34

A girl can be psychologically damaged if she is so betrayed when in love. She may never trust a man again.

A boy who says "I love you" just to get laid, is just as much a deceitful thief as a crooked accountant.

Both have committed fraud.

The woman who falls pregnant deliberately, hoping to get married, or at least gain child support, is deceitful as well.

 A con-artist is a patient chameleon.

Spin and Relativism

To the fraudster, it is part of the game of life. The practice of deception in the corporate world is no different.

What makes it easier for people to justify their behavior is actually society's acceptance of relative values.

Australia is notorious for accepting sporting heroes' poor behavior, yet we still call them role models. At the other extreme, Americans are shocked when a politician's immorality is exposed. Why?

Ironically, when enough time has passed, these figures are often remembered as "lovable rogues".

How stupid to expect an athlete to teach your child anything more than the fun of athletics. How stupid to purchase an electrical appliance because a footballer says it's good. How naïve to expect a person who is charismatic and popular enough to gain public office, also has moral fiber.

Leaders should be good leaders; but they are also frail humans who are just as vulnerable to temptation as the next person.

Serial liars rarely admit that what they did was wrong. Often they are sorry they were caught and regret they tried to con someone who turned out to be "difficult to deal with".

It is human nature to be tempted to put a "spin" on our mistakes.

Adam put a spin on his disobedience in the Garden of Eden by blaming Eve, who then blamed the serpent for deceiving her. Both failed to take responsibility for their actions. In that story, the serpent was the "con-artist" but there was a price to pay for the man and the woman being foolish and self-indulgent.

Men and women have been blaming each other ever since!

The most successful "spin" is the philosophy of "relativism", the idea that there is no empirical right and wrong.

In the late 20th century the idea of right and wrong being in the eye of the beholder, took root in our education system. Just like in the "Values Clarification" game, where the value of a person is determined by how much benefit they are.

The victims are considered dispensable players in the game and therefore it is their own fault if they do not wake up to what is going on. It is indeed the "evolution" of the survival of the fittest.

When that philosophy is combined with the trendy New Age idea of "whatever you want your truth to be is fine," there is no place left for accountability. One person can deceive another and believe they have done nothing wrong.

Here is where it gets interesting. If truth is a relative term, then fraud is only fraud in the eye of the victim.

Clearly we know this is not true, however, the fraudster will tell you he is not a bad person. Often he loves his family and he abhors violence. However, the world hasn't done him any favors and anything he gains is considered "fair game."

In his own eyes, his obligation is to him and his own.

The con-artist sees his victims as valuable only as long as they are of use to him financially.

36

What If They Do Look Different?

Just to add to the confusion, we've also been instructed by political correctness, to not stereotype those who look different, or have values that are not the same as ours.

The problem is that sometimes people present themselves a certain way because they have issues!

Why shouldn't we be suspicious of someone who wears a tee-shirt with an abusive message on it? What is motivating them?

It is true that people who dress threateningly may well be dangerous, but the biggest deception is to believe that we are sufficiently good judges of character to protect ourselves, without doing proper due-diligence.

Why are "lovely girls" attracted to "bad men" who eventually mistreat them? The warning signs are usually there, but love or low self-esteem or rebellion; allow them to fall prey to a manipulator.

Given time a "charming young rogue" may just turn out to be an immature, selfish manipulator.

In Summary

Next time you think about employing or romancing someone, really take the time to think about why they may be projecting the image they are. Is it individualism, rebellion or is it really too good to be true?

Certainly don't only judge a book by its cover, but remember a book cover is designed to attract the kind of reader the author wants.

Take the Princess Warrior Challenge...

\ Have you ever been attracted to someone but your friends warned you it would be a bad idea?

\ Were they right?

\ Were they wrong?

\ More importantly, why were they right or wrong?

\ Have you experienced conflict between your heart and your head? Write down pros and cons to each argument and look inside yourself for reasons why you may have made a poor choice.

Chapter Four

How do Predators Choose their Prey?

Q: How can you tell if you are vulnerable to a potential fraud?

A: By believing it won't happen to you! A predator in the wild generally looks for a potential meal by watching for stray herd members. When an animal becomes separated from its herd it loses the protection that comes from the collective senses.

A Predator...

A predator does not have to be violent to violate someone, nor do they have to behave like wild animals. What makes us vulnerable?

Pride...

"Pride goes before destruction and a haughty spirit before a fall"

Proverbs 16:18

Con-artists love prideful people because they only have to rely on flattery to manipulate them, using phrases like:

"This kind of investment is not for everyone...only the truly clever can understand how great it is...the public will never be wealthy like us... this information is only accessible to certain people..."

In the arena of romance, flattery and adoration are addictive to someone who wants to be loved.

A con-artist offers relief, even "escape".

Low Self-Esteem...

This is the other side of the pride coin. A person starved of self-esteem will be like a parched traveler offered a refreshing drink.

The adoration and flattery that a scammer uses will go straight to the heart of the victim who will want more. Before long, they will give anything to please the person who appears to be satisfying their need. Eventually the scammer uses the threat of leaving to elicit more from their victim.

When the victim is bled dry, they are abandoned.

Busyness...

A busy person is more likely to become a victim of fraud.

Why?

A busy person is often stressed and over-worked. Stress is a major cause of depression.

In our modern society being stressed and over-worked has become normal.

How often does someone ask you, "How are things going... busy?"

"Oh yes, busy, busy, busy!" Why do we wear busyness like a badge of honor?

Or the phone call, "Look, I know you're busy but..."

Anyone with children and who works outside the home is considered busy. Ironically, the stay-at-home mum is often viewed as having taken the easy option. I don't share this view. Anyone who has been home with three small children knows how draining it can be.

A busy person will often be grateful for the expertise of others. It may sound like an ideal scenario to delegate investigating an opportunity to someone else. However, if your money is important to you, you need to follow things up yourself.

It's no use blaming someone else if it doesn't work out.

Many leaders have fallen into that trap.

I suggest we look closer at the possibility that it is not busyness but in fact mental laziness that motivated us to let someone else do the work.

Such an attitude is simple pride... and not the good kind.

> Don't be so self-important that you cannot take the time to make a responsible decision.

Time management is a lot easier than you might think.

It starts with the ability to say "no" to new projects or "good-bye" to existing ones in order to make room for new ones.

As Oprah famously said, "You can have it all, just not all at the same time!" If you don't have time to think and reflect on people and opportunities, you will not make a considered decision.

A con offers to feed our dream of the life we'd really like to live. It could be in how to make passive income so that we can stop being so busy. It could be the promise of romance, "if you like pina coladas, and getting caught in the rain... making love at midnight... in the dunes of the cape"...sorry, that song carries me away.

The truth is, romance is great but there are warning signs. Most normal men run out of flowers pretty early in the relationship. Most gave up writing poetry after college when they started writing work reports.

If a man is acting too much like a hero, ask more questions because he either has an agenda or he could be gay! (They are the only ones who read the same romance novels you did!)

41

Victims of fraud are no more stupid than the average person. Predators target people who reveal a need.

Predators do not target the stupid or the clever, they do not target people because they are women or men or of a particular race, religion or job description.

Wittingly or unwittingly, our conversation and body language reveal what is important to us. We reveal our desires, our goals and our past, to a sympathetic ear.

It's easy to judge fraud victims for being greedy, but who knows how anyone would react when the answers to their needs are presented in a persuasive way?

Predators look for people with needs. Then they tailor themselves as the answer to those needs.

Too Good to be True?

You've heard the saying, "if it sounds too good to be true, it probably is!" In spite of its kernel of truth, I find that saying irritating and small minded because it is the ultimate dream stealing statement...

Consider:

- There was a time when a woman owning her own business sounded too good to be true (depending on your perspective).
- A horseless carriage – too good to be true.
- A flying machine – too good to be true.
- An information superhighway – again, too good to be true.
- What about salvation for sin by one man's sacrifice? Millions of sensible people believe it.
- A God whose Presence can be felt?

Entrepreneurs have always believed in dreams that others said sounded "too good to be true".

It's how Multi-level Marketing businesses grow. Many of their members succeed because they believe what others consider impossible.

Sometimes their dreams work out and sometimes not.

What one person considers too good to be true, another has faith in.

This is why we believe "The Dream". A con-artist presents a fairly plausible explanation of how a project will work, it feeds our dream of a financial breakthrough, and we are already warm to the idea.

Unfortunately this faith is open to manipulation. That is why many church people are often vulnerable to fraud.

It's not because they are stupid or ignorant. It is because they are used to believing what others don't.

When you have experienced the miraculous, it makes it easier to believe that the opportunity is a miracle. Good, honest people, religious or not, generally have friends who share their values.

 When you are used to dealing with people who tell the truth, you are less likely to question what someone tells you about what they do for a living.

Wolves among Sheep

It is therefore easy for wolves to get among the sheep. All they have to do is look like a sheep, talk like a sheep and wear clothes like a sheep.

If you've been defrauded by someone claiming to be religious, instead of labeling the whole group "hypocrites", consider that wolves in sheep's clothing are going to talk like and act like the other sheep.

43

Sincere Christians are generous givers. They also have faith in God's blessing because they have experienced it.

It is not a stretch for them to believe that an opportunity is the blessing of God in their lives. Being generous makes way for abundance. However, poor management can intercept blessing.

Christians, Jews and Muslims have been persecuted for centuries, yet their faith sustains them. They have an ability to bounce back that people without faith, do not.

"The Secret"

Those who adhere to the popular teachings of "The Secret" are another faith group likely to be taken advantage of.

"The Secret" phenomenon has attracted devotees all over the world.

Why? It offers a strategy for a person to get whatever they want. It promises to answer a "need".

Adherents of "The Secret" believe in The Law of Attraction. It is the idea that whatever happens to a person is the result of their thoughts. By projecting their thoughts out to the universe, they believe they will attract what they are thinking about into their lives.

Of course there is more to it than just thinking. Goal setting, visualization, affirmations and effort are all strategies for "attracting" what you want into your life. The principles that move circumstances in your life are universal, but they are not subject to a neat formula that exempts you from adversity.

 Without wisdom wealth walks.

This faith-based philosophy can make people open to suggestion from unscrupulous people posing as the "Deliverer" of whatever they put out there.

Finance and love are at the top of most people's lists. The twin desires for more money and to be loved are very powerful emotions for a predator to manipulate.

Gravity is a law. It works all the time. A principle works in general, but variables can alter the outcome. For example, smiling at someone will generally produce a smile in response, but it may not.

The Law of Attraction is really a Principle.

The Law of Attraction is called a "Law" because it's a catchier marketing term. It is true that when you focus on something and put your energy towards it, you will generally find yourself moving closer to it. However, there is no guarantee that any specific opportunity is going to work out.

Neither God nor the "Universe" will back up a bad judgment call, although the Lord promises to turn the sorrows of those who trust Him, into joy. Once again, note the proviso. Do not lose faith because your expectations of what "should" have happened were disappointed.

By the way, from a scientific perspective, it is more often true that "Opposites Attract". From magnetic positive and negative energy fields to unscientific "love", the attraction of opposites is more likely. However, science does not stretch this principle to say that being nasty will attract goodness into your life!

You are more likely to find positive opportunities coming to you if you are diligent and can be trusted with that opportunity!

What We Really Desire is – Satisfaction

Satisfaction is a sense of fulfillment or contentment. We want to feel happy with ourselves and content with our lives.

The media constantly presents us with something claiming to be better or more exciting than what we have. Why? Money, of course! We spend and the media get paid for the advertising. Unfortunately the answer to our needs is not in chasing love or money.

Satisfaction: a Perspective, Not a Goal

Hence, satisfaction will be ever elusive to those who seek it in increased material gain or in another relationship. Lonely single parents are easy targets for smooth talking predators, male or female.

Society often judges "silly" single mothers for falling for one bad egg after another. However, loneliness is one of the most powerful motivators in the world.

Is her longing for satisfaction any less deserving than ours?

A person with a damaged self-esteem to start with, will often tolerate poor behavior because they do not want to be alone. At some point the person they love was kind enough to them to offer some hope of a better future.

In years gone by, a courtship was a time of finding out whether two people would want to spend the rest of their lives together. Their engagement was a time of preparation for the marriage. After the wedding the couple moved in together. By then they knew each other and their families also knew each other quite well.

The Chocolate Complex

The problem with the freedom modern society affords is the chocolate complex:

A little is good

Therefore more must be better

Stuffing me silly without restraint must be bliss.

Why do I feel so sick...?

When we think we are in love and the chemistry is bubbling, we want to be with that person all of the time. They are satisfying a need within us and it's normal to want to keep that feeling going.

What better way to maintain that feeling than by moving in together as quickly as we can, so we can be enjoying that "feeling" non-stop?

There is a problem with such hasty behavior. There is no time to get to know the whole person before moving in together, which takes emotional commitment up a notch. It requires commitment to utility bills, respecting a previous partner's access rights to the new partner's children, sharing household responsibilities etc.

Quite often we don't just move in with someone who interests us, we buy into a whole complicated network of relationships and commitments.

It is a mistake to expect other family members to treat him like a brother or son-in-law before they've had a chance to get to know him.

 A romantic predator answers a need for love and when the person is hooked, proceeds to take advantage of them.

Oops!

It's often quoted that at least one in four women has been sexually abused. If that happened in childhood how can that little girl grow up with healthy expectations of love? A victim is often reluctant to end a relationship because of the crumbs they are receiving, and even holds the dream that things will improve.

Similarly, towards the end of a financial scam, victims are often reluctant to believe that whoever had been answering their financial need to date is a fraud.

Disentangling yourself from such a relationship once the passion fizzles or you discover he is a lunatic, is expensive, emotionally taxing and possibly dangerous. A six-month romp could cost you half of all your assets!

The time spent together will also have an effect on whether there are legal and financial obligations as a de facto couple. It can vary from state to state.

> "To accept it is a fraud would mean accepting that there is no more hope of money being returned."

What about the Business Arena?

Emotionally healthy women can say "no" because that's what they want. They are not emotionally manipulated. Emotionally healthy women have a good self-esteem that attracts respect.

> We can be strong in one area and weak in another. Business success can go to our heads.

Sarah was a gifted businesswoman in New Zealand. She owned her own agency and was the leader of a local club. She was an avid property investor and a role model for her female staff. People would ask her advice on what they should do to be as successful.

Other clubs invited her to talk to members about her strategies for success. It was an exciting, heady time.

Sarah was not a fraud, but a fraudster used her influence to gain customers for his property investment scam.

Unfortunately, she began to believe her own press.

Sarah became so full of herself that when Kate, a "mere" receptionist, mentioned she was considering buying a house, Sarah declared "Take me to see it and I'll tell you if you should buy it or not!" She was oblivious to the younger woman's jaw dropping.

The boundary of authority was clearly overstepped, but fortunately Kate did not let that influence her decision. It did however, cause her to put some distance into their relationship and go on to find another job.

Kate later told me, "There is a difference between respecting a person's opinion and giving them control over your decisions." Unfortunately, Sarah continued to believe her own press. Her self-esteem was so high that she was overconfident about her ability to succeed and her ability to discern a good deal.

Consequently, she was conned, lost several properties and considerable money. Her confidence in herself was, in fact, pride that blinded her to her fallibility.

To make matters worse, her followers also lost money as they had relied on her recommendation. Her job description was in one area of people's lives. She should not have tried to influence them in areas where she had no business.

We cannot judge Sarah too harshly though. I too know what it is like to have people rely on my due-diligence for their financial decisions and things have not worked out. It is very painful for everyone.

At some point, Sarah's followers have to take responsibility for their own lack of investigation. Once again, busy people were happy to rely on someone else's due-diligence.

> Lust and the lust for wealth blind us to risks and their consequences.

Financial idolatry not only deceived Sarah, but also those following her who should have thought for themselves and taken responsibility for their investment decisions.

Delegating or Dumping?

Megan and Susan were a sister team in Sacramento who created a company that networked businesses. However, they were growing so rapidly they decided to consult with a business coach. The coach proceeded to reshape their business.

However, there was little actual improvement to the business and a lot of unaccountable hours of work were invoiced.

One of the things the coach insisted on was that a lot of money be spent on advertising. Coincidentally, the coach's girlfriend designed the ads. Ads, by the way, that were never completed.

The coach had actually been stealing Megan and Susan's intellectual property, undermining their customers' confidence as well as milking any profits that were made.

Megan and Susan will tell you that they delegated too much and did not have adequate accountability measures in place. Today, however, their business is going strong.

Networking

One of the ways we can minimize risk is by connecting with other businesspeople so we can share ideas and experiences that help us grow.

We can also share our knowledge of someone who has done the wrong thing. While I don't endorse gossip that undermines reputation, shared knowledge can save the same expensive lesson from being repeated.

Consider joining both women's and mixed networking groups. Subscribe to newsletters and go along to workshops and talks on topics that will help you.

Much of my due-diligence is done as I meet people at events and ask for their intelligence about someone.

The next step is to do searches on the internet and even employ the services of a professional investigator to do a background check, if necessary.

Take the Princess Warrior Challenge...

- Have you ever compromised your values to get what you want either emotionally or in business?

- How did that make you feel?

- What have you purchased that you did not particularly want just to impress others?

- Do you think you can be free of the need to impress?

- What wisdom would you like to pass on to your children in regards to being true to themselves while pursuing their goals?

Part 2:

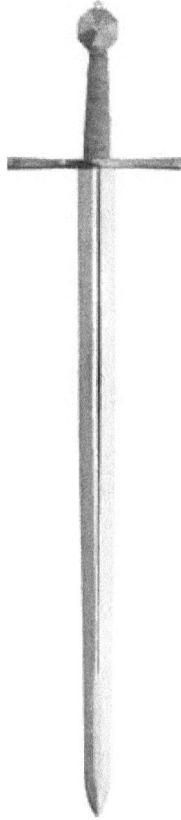

EN GARDE!

Chapter Five

The Double-edged Sword

The double-edged sword is especially useful in battle as it cuts both ways.

The diagram on the next page shows the various parts, and then we will examine what they symbolize.

Tung

Pommel

Hilt

Grip

Cross guard

Ricasso

Fuller

Tip

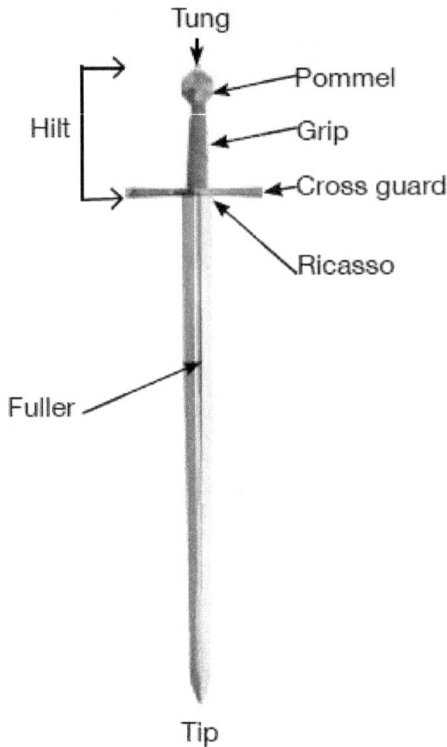

Wealth is a double-edged sword.

Over centuries, the sword has been refined to become a weapon of beauty, balance and retribution.

A sword is a tool of the warrior.

The warrior is not the sword, although his or her skilled swordsmanship may make it appear that one is an extension of the other!

I interviewed James of "War Sword" a shop that sells all kinds of swords from medieval broadswords to Luke Skywalker's light-saber, along with various historical helmets. It's a history buff's fantasy.

James is an expert on swords and their history. He informed me that each part of the sword has a purpose, and educated me on the intricacies of the various aspects of the double-edged sword.

I started this chapter with the metaphor of wealth being a sword that cuts both ways, symbolic of being put to good use as well as bringing out the worst in people. James' expert knowledge sheds a whole new light on the subject. Each part of the sword corresponds with an aspect of our wealth, sometimes used for creation, sometimes used for destruction. Each requires learning, patience, discipline and skill.

The sword has a sharp end for effectively piercing through resistance, just like wealth can open doors and get things done quickly. Private health insurance is a good example of wealth which is able to get a person further ahead in the queue, of what is loosely called the health system.

 Like the sword, our wealth can cut both ways. It can do great things for us and it can also make us vulnerable.

The Pommel

The Pommel counterbalances the sword. It is spherical in shape and quite often has a small knob (tung) at the top. In close combat, the sword could be swung up and around so that when the warrior was in close contact he could strike his enemy on the head with the pommel for maximum damage. This is where we get the verb to "pummel" someone. It means "to beat".

The strength of the sword lies in the fact that the blade is one continuous piece right through the handle to the "tung." This small button is the back-up strategy. It is not going to fall off and therefore represents your backup plan. When you get too close to a deal and find that it's not what you thought, it's important to have an exit or back-up strategy. Doing business with friends often turns out to be a bad idea and can destroy a close friendship. A back-up plan to extricate you from an uncomfortably close situation is important.

James proceeded to demonstrate how a medieval soldier would swing his sword around at close range in order to bash in the head of his opponent. "Nice." I commented.

> When creating a business plan, ask yourself:
>
> "What if our partnership does not work out?"

Butchered friendship

Dennis managed a butcher shop in Dallas but had run into some bad luck, became unemployed and then personally bankrupt. Jenny had always bought her meat from Dennis and over the years they chatted on and off about what went on in each other's lives.

Consequently, Dennis had accumulated knowledge about Jenny's investment properties and her desire to be in business one day. Dennis assured Jenny that his hard luck was not his fault and that he could run a butcher shop better than his boss any day.

Dennis suggested he could help Jenny fulfill her desire to own a business. She should buy two butcher shops and they would be partners. He would run them because he had the expertise.

Well two months on, Jenny had not seen a Profit and Loss Statement, nor did she have access to online bank accounts. It seemed all the money she had invested was going out in "expenses". The only money going into the bank account was via a check or credit card payment which was unusual, as other such shops had a high percentage of cash sales.

> Jenny had not been assertive at the start and did not put controls in place that would protect her interest.

When she occasionally queried Dennis he would sound hurt and defensive. After all, he "was the one slaving his guts out while she sat back and enjoyed the profits!"

The only problem was that her share of the profits was not forthcoming, but he managed to upgrade his car and lifestyle!

Jenny has now employed a consultant to put monitoring measures in place for greater accountability. It may be that the business will be put into administration until the profit and loss is fully audited.

Jenny had actually been carried away by someone feeding her dream. She loved the idea of being a business owner, but was reluctant to do the "boring bits" of due-diligence and having proper agreements drawn up. She chose to trust her long time "friend", but really she didn't want to upset and offend him.

If you feel you cannot confront issues for whatever reason, you should read it as a BIG WARNING SIGNAL!

> An unequal balance of psychological power is destructive in normal friendships and disastrous in business.

The Grip

The grip of the sword is the place of control. If gripped too tightly, the sword becomes unwieldy and the swordsman cannot take advantage of the full range of the sword's capabilities. If gripped loosely, there is a strong possibility that at the first encounter it will simply be knocked out of the hand attempting to hold it.

> A smart person, regardless of their level of wealth, has a firm grip.

Your swordsmanship in business and in life will determine the material and emotional success you have. It is not just for battle.

Your wealth is not just about accumulating. It can also protect the vulnerable. I am involved with an organization that sponsors an orphanage and a rescue home in Cambodia. They rescue girls from the sex-slave industry.

Apart from sustaining the girls, the finances are used where possible to rescue girls from brothel owners. The "working" girls begin servicing men from the age of 5 with fellatio, until they are able to be used with greater versatility.

Thanks to a number of dedicated groups, young Cambodian girls can have a better future. Wealth can protect us from the harsh realities of life. However, it is far more satisfying to use it to soften the harshness of someone else's life.

Holding a sword too tightly will not allow you to maneuver it effectively. It won't leave your hand, but neither will it be truly effective.

 Wealth gripped tightly will not grow or do anything useful.

Many people want to be wealthy but will not spend a cent on their education. Many people selling their house want top dollar, but are not willing to invest in marketing. They also want a bargain when repurchasing in the same market!

Fear

Fear often dominates a stingy spirit. Once bitten, twice shy. When you've been burned in business it's easy to give up. It is also easy to let one person from a group set your opinion of the entire group. I've heard it said that "Christians are stingy". Statistically however, this is not true.

A 2008 report on ABC Network's 20/20 program, investigated who were the biggest givers in the USA and who were the most selfish. Religious people were not only the biggest givers to their particular organization, but they are also the biggest givers to non-religious charities.

Who were the stingiest? They were those who worked on Wall Street. Does that make all rich people selfish? Of course not! It might mean that certain groups have prevailing philosophies that affect their generosity.

Perhaps it's not money but greed that influences a culture. Greed will make you more vulnerable to fraud. It is very important to search it out in your heart and be honest with yourself. Are you too frightened to give generously?

> Some people are so selfish they wouldn't spit on you if your head was on fire!

Too Loose?

If your grip is loose and you are not paying attention to what is in your hand, a sword can easily be dropped, knocked out or simply and discreetly removed from your possession.

Successful people are not always aware of where their money is going. The area of vulnerability for this group is deception. Keeping up with the latest trends can have a detrimental effect on a bank balance and increase stress.

They may know they are investing with a person, but may place a higher level of trust in that person than they ought.

Highly successful people are very aware of what their money is doing. Their money, like their grip, is balanced. They investigate to confirm, not only where the money will be going, but the person through whom it will go.

> "Pay the government what you must, but for goodness' sake, don't tip them, they're not doing a good enough job!"

(Kerry Packer, media magnate who, at the time of his death, was the richest and arguably the most influential man in Australia.)

The Cross Guard

The sword also has a cross guard. It sits between the base of the sword and the grip. Its purpose is two-fold:

1. It protects the hand wielding the sword against oncoming blades.

2. It prevents the hand from sliding down the blade and being sliced by its own weapon.

The cross guard represents protection and caution. It is fixed into place. It does not move its boundary when pressured. It is also positioned before the part that is the danger zone, not half way down where is it too late to be effective.

It is important to have safeguards in your life and business that are areas of NO COMPROMISE. These boundaries should be positioned well before the danger zone.

When it comes to romance, have some boundaries preset so that when you find yourself attracted to someone, you don't have a head full of passion when asked to make a decision. Consider having a set of criteria the person must fit before you hand over your money or your heart.

A good financial advisor should be able to assess an investment and warn you of its pitfalls. Likewise, friends may caution you about your new boyfriend's history of womanizing.

A checklist of warning signals is a very handy way to shortlist the opportunity or romance. These will be explored later. Given enough experiences, your heart will become a confused, rough beach that no-one can comfortably enjoy.

Every person you become involved with leaves tracks across your heart. Each set of tracks will leave bumps that the next person will have to walk over.

The Ricasso

This is an area at the base of the blade and in front of the cross guard. It is does not have sharp edges. Its purpose is to enable the wielder to safely place the other hand on the blade as it swings around for greater maneuverability.

It is a very dangerous place as it is only wide enough to allow one hand to grip. The cautions have been assessed and dismissed and the person is prepared to take the final risk. Maybe it will pay off and maybe one small knock will slice the hand open.

This could be symbolic of a last chance.

The Fuller

The fuller is a very important aspect of the sword.

"So this allows the blood to escape while the blade is in your enemy's body?" I asked, referring to the groove carved out down the length of the blade.

"Many people assume that," James answered. "But that is not its true purpose. The fuller is a groove that has been dug out in order to lighten the sword."

Suddenly I understood so much more about myself.

The groove of the fuller makes the sword lighter and less wearisome on the arm. However, it also makes the blade rigid and easier to direct.

James demonstrated with a piece of paper. He waved the paper around showing how it was easily bent and very unresponsive to his hand's direction. Then he folded the paper down the middle and held it at one end at the groove created by the fold. When he waved it again the paper was quite rigid and followed the direction of his hand.

"That's amazing!" I gasped, "We can't fight effectively if our personal issues are weighing us down!"

"You are starting to sound like Oprah," muttered James.

"Do you think she'd have me?" I asked the expert swordsman as I wielded the glinting blade that fascinated me.

It's so true.

We must shed unnecessary hang-ups and past memories that weigh us down.

It is important to find a way to turn the bad things that have happened to us, things that have weakened us, into things that make us better.

When we stop carrying the burdens of the past, we are no longer tired and can notice the future ahead. An easier burden means we will be better able to wield our wealth sword.

Excess weight in your wealth sword can also represent unnecessary expenses.

Review your cash flow regularly in order to make sure you are only paying for what you need to. Check insurance policies in case you are paying twice, especially disability insurance.

Are there sufficient workplace health and safety policies implemented to minimize the risk of claims that increase insurance premiums? Is your workplace cover appropriate? Do you have fewer staff than when you first took out your policy?

Consider the work vehicles. Are they economical? Did you choose them merely to impress? Does your business return justify the expense? Are you paying for perks that your employees are not using?

Consider joining a peer mentoring group to get ideas on what other businesspeople find effective. There are consultants who can go through all your expenses and make recommendations that will save money.

Out-sourcing is very popular now. Why have a full-time bookkeeper, when there might be only 10 hours of actual bookkeeping work to do?

> A dollar saved is better than a dollar earned because you don't pay tax on it.

10 Wealth Lessons:

From The Double-edged Sword

1. It cuts both ways - Wealth can do a lot of good e.g. helping people, but can also create problems. Money doesn't change people. It brings out what they are really like, good or bad, strong character or weak. Its loss magnifies who they are.

2. It has a protective cross guard to prevent your hand slipping onto the blade – it's what holds us back from danger. It's important to place boundaries in your financial life that protect you from your own eagerness.

3. The size must fit the person wielding it. If it's too heavy, you might be tempted to let it drop, or someone can deceive you into letting them hold it. A sword that is too small speaks of an inadequate tool for the job required. Sometimes you do just need more money!

4. If you are not content, you are managing out of fear or greed and there will never be an amount of money to satisfy you. Achieving your goals will feel hollow instead of

satisfying. Don't be discouraged, contentment is an attitude that can be learned. It's a lot like patience.

5. Quality over ostentation. You only need one sword but it should be a good one.

6. Maintenance – The sword must be oiled, prepared for battle, and afterward must be cleaned. Keep honest records and a clear conscience. Otherwise, cross contamination will affect you.

7. Learning and practice. Read widely, keep up to date in your field of expertise, listen to CDs, visit great websites, join networking groups and think critically.

8. It must be held firmly, but not too tightly. Clutching it hard will result in poor performance, too loose and it will fall away from you.

9. Be prepared to give it up. It is a tool, not an idol. Treat it like a tool and you will not be heartbroken when it is taken from you. Tools are replaceable, you'll get another one. You will know how to use other skills and implements. The new won't fit with the old.

10. Warriors are adaptable. One of the best books I've read on change is Who Moved My Cheese? By Dr. Spencer Johnson. If you choose the way you respond to change, then no matter what comes your way, you will cope and even thrive.

Take the Warrior Princess Challenge...

- What has happened in your life to create excess emotional or financial weight?

- Which parts of your business correspond to the various parts of the double-edged sword?

- What criteria are important to you in a man or a business associate?

- Can you measure these criteria without revealing what you are looking for to the person of interest?

- Would you like to learn more about real swords?

- Visit James' website: www.warsword.com.au.

Chapter Six

The Mind Behind The Sword

The problem with deception is that the one under deception does not know they are being deceived.

In life, in business and in faith, we need a sure foundation before we step forward. Contrary to popular belief, truth is not relative.

Have you heard the one about the accountant's interview?

> When interviewing an accountant, simply ask "What is two plus two?"
>
> Hire the one who answers, "Whatever you want it to be!"

Sorry, the truth is true whether we like it or not.

The money is either there or it isn't.

The first step to protecting our minds is to move away from the belief that truth is what we want it to be.

A deceived person cannot see the truth, they just think they can.

This can be heartbreaking for the families of people who are being fleeced by a Romeo or Nigerian scam. Sadly there is no crime until there is a complaint from the victim who may be quite willing to go on giving money to their new "friend" or email correspondent.

The key is: always be prepared to consider other possibilities without being so open minded that any rubbish can fall in.

The Helmet – Protect your Mind

In addition to a sword, warriors wear a helmet. It protects the brain, the thought-life. Do you think about what you think about? Have you considered where your thought-life might take you?

Ross Abraham is a well known minister and speaker, but he was once my youth leader. I still remember writing down the words he said that impacted me:

"Sow a thought and reap an action

Sow an action and reap a habit

Sow a habit and reap a lifestyle

Sow a lifestyle and reap a destiny..."

You have probably heard the saying, "You are what you eat". Perhaps you have also heard, "As a man thinks in his heart, so is he."

There are plenty of books and motivational speakers telling you to visualize what you want and it will come to you, but rarely do they warn you of the danger of destructive visualization.

Goals and visualization have their place but it's the little daily thoughts that make us who we are.

When we control our thoughts, we are able to analyze what goes through them more objectively. As a result we reduce the risk of deception.

How?

Reality Check

✓ Do you get angry quickly?

✓ Do you stew over a past conversation?

✓ Does remembering something cause you to become angry?

✓ Do you take your bad day out on your family?

When Hitler began taking over other European countries, England's Prime Minister, Neville Chamberlain, adopted a policy of appeasement. Why? No-one wanted another war. Winston Churchill's warning cries went unheeded and were even ridiculed.

People didn't want to believe Hitler's strategy of expansion had sinister undertones. It was Poland's alliance with Britain that interrupted Hitler's conquest.

> Know when to draw the line. Don't keep making excuses (appeasement) for suspect behavior.

Baby boomers are often caught out because they are facing retirement and realizing they do not have enough money for it. Financial deception requires not only that the investor believes the scheme to be true, but that he wants to believe it.

A scheme is offered that they want to believe in, so half the persuasion can be self-induced. It is important to be able to walk away from the table.

> When we want to believe something we become blind to danger signals.

Taking Your Thoughts Captive!

A helmet protects the warrior's head.

Do you protect your mind?

How many times are we admonished to be "open-minded"? It is important to develop discernment, to carefully consider what is being presented before accepting it.

Think about this. It has been suggested that art imitated life, and then life began to imitate art. The conclusion could be made that art now dictates life!

Is it within the realm of possibility that artists and the media are telling our society how to live?

Possibly. After all, why should we buy anything unrelated to sport, just because an athlete says it's a great idea? Why is the media more interested in reporting on the alcohol consumption of our grand final winners than on the victory itself?

What has this to do with protecting against fraud?

It is your thoughts that create your lifestyle.

Filter what is Seen and Heard

Audiences are addicted to soap operas because they want to follow the next romance. There are no "happy ever afters" on a TV series.

I remember enjoying the sexual tension building on a popular TV drama. However, once the first couple fell in love, or rather into bed, had a fight and made up, instead of creating interesting storylines about their lives together, they had to break up so the audience could become hooked on another "will they, won't they" scenario. It's not healthy viewing.

Successful people understand the importance of feeding their mind good food. Inspirational movies make us feel like we too can make the world a better place.

Beware of the movie playing in your mind as well. I used to be one who stewed on things. I wasn't very big or strong and I hated conflict. I felt angry at my perceived powerlessness. Since childhood I would stew on things rather than address them or let them go. I would rehearse arguments in my mind and come up with brilliant answers. I stewed over resentments. I pondered the great questions of the universe.

> **Whatever the mind conceives and invokes with emotions, the body will exhibit.**

I didn't understand that a person becomes what they think about; that I could control my thought-life.

I daydreamed about the boy I had a crush on who didn't notice me. I was lucky because I didn't get "lucky".

The James Dean "cool rebel" type might have been an exciting boyfriend, but is likely to be a serious risk in business and as a life partner. I'd had school friends who had accidentally fallen pregnant. They didn't mean to, it just happened. In spite of knowing where babies came from since primary school, these intelligent girls didn't seem to make the connection...well, a connection was made all right, but not one they had anticipated!

Things had started with a thought.

A daydream.

A suggestion.

Then in my twenties I learned about taking my thoughts captive.

Uncontrolled thoughts of love and romance will give a girl unrealistic expectations. This can actually be to the detriment of her adult relationship with her spouse.

Uncontrolled thoughts of promiscuity and lust will make a man or woman more vulnerable to cheating.

Beware of developing a "crush" on the person or company you want to do business with. If you want them more than they want you; you are immediately at a disadvantage.

> **As actions are the result of your thoughts, you can and should choose what you think about!**

What Are You Thinking?

Understanding your thought pattern about yourself and how an opportunity or relationship will pan out, determines whether you are in control of your decisions or you are being manipulated by your own desires or someone else's.

According to the popular teaching of The Secret, your thoughts create your world. I agree. Your thoughts have caused you to make choices bringing you to where you are today - but they did not make bad things happen to you.

That kind of thinking is, at best, superficial and at worst offensive. It blames the victim.

You did not attract rape with your thought life. Your negativity did not attract the bushfire that burned down your home. Sometimes bad things happen to good people.

> True champions are not those whose thoughts are so positive that nothing bad happens to them.

You may have been naïve. You may have been too trusting. Yet trust is not a bad attribute in a person. Without trust there can be no love. It is your response to adversity that produces the victory and that is determined by your attitude and the support network you draw on.

No-one is an island. I could not have recovered from my disaster without carefully chosen friends and putting my hand up when it got too much.

> True champions are those whose thought-life helps them to get up again after taking a hit.

I remember waking up each morning with tremors running down my legs from terror, dry-retching as the horror of what had happened returned to me. All day, butterflies would torment my stomach and I was loath to check my emails in case there was a nasty one waiting for me.

When I couldn't even think of what to feed my family while gazing into the pantry, I decided I had to do whatever it took to get through the situation.

I had three small children and a husband to consider. I didn't want my girls to grow up needing counseling because mommy was incapacitated and weeping uncontrollably.

So, I was sensible. I went to my doctor and began taking medication that allowed me to think more clearly. I deliberately avoided people who could steal my joy. I made myself go to a women's social group to make new friends.

I prayed, and prayed, and prayed.

I remember parking in a dark street one night and screaming at God, the names of the people who were suffering.

I was crying out for answers, as I had really thought the opportunity was His blessing in my life.

Quietly in my heart, I felt one of His answers. Each person is having their own experience. What they are going through is between them and Me. I know what is best.

I had to realize that I was not anyone else's "fixer".

Nobody wants a "Joseph experience". Remember Joseph? He had the coat of many colors. He was the guy whose brothers sold into slavery and just when things were looking up, he landed in prison for many years.

However, he ended up impressing the Pharaoh and became 2IC of Egypt.

Some people fight and fight and break through. I found my breakthrough in surrender.

Once I faced the worst case scenario and accepted its possibility, the fear seemed to dissolve. Occasionally it would flare up, but the sting was gone.

I could smile at the future once more. I was reminded of an ancient verse (Psalm 91:14-16) I had come across while waiting for our money to return, just before I found out it was gone.

Such verses breathe life into me, especially when I personalize them as below. Perhaps they will for you too.

> 14 *"Because she has set her love upon Me, therefore I will deliver her; I will set her on high, because she has known My name.*
>
> 15 *She shall call upon Me, and I will answer her; I will be with her in trouble; I will deliver her and honor her.*
>
> 16 *With long life I will satisfy her, And show her My salvation."*

Choose ahead of time to be optimistic without being naïve. You are only a victim if you choose to be.

As the saying goes,

> **"Fool me once, shame on you.**
>
> **Fool me twice, shame on me."**

Even if you have blown it time after time after time, it is possible to change your future by right thinking!

Get some therapy to heal the memories of horrible things that have tainted your thought processes.

Find your faith, sit quietly and do business with your Maker. Imagine taking the painful memory and placing it in His hands. Ask Him to fill that empty space in your heart.

Dwelling on the past is not healthy. Once you have keys for dealing with those memories, then it's time to build your future.

Start by thinking about your circumstances in a visual way. This could be picturing how you want your business to be running or visualizing the way your relationship could be.

Then assess what it looks like now.

The next step: Analyze the size and nature of the gap that lies between them.

Who is the Me I want to Be?

1. How would the person you want to become think about a situation?
2. How would she decide on a business deal?
3. What kind of questions does she ask?
4. What kind of wife or partner is she?
5. How do people respond to her?
6. What is it about her that garners respect?
7. How does she dress?
8. How does she speak?
9. How does she treat those who are not as "together" as she is?
10. How does her partner speak about her?
11. How do her children speak about her?
12. How would her friends describe her?

If you have found that pondering these questions has left you feeling discouraged, take heart. Life is a journey, you don't change overnight. Be patient and try doing just one thing from your list.

As a young woman I smoked a little bit. I never saw myself as a smoker, just someone who smoked occasionally. It was easy for me to quit. Heavy smokers are identified as smokers. Do you see the identity problem?

> You are not a loser trying to do things better, you are a winner who occasionally "stuffs up".

You don't have to be good at everything. You do have to be true to yourself. Work out your strengths and weaknesses and accept them. If you have an area of weakness that is destructive, care enough about yourself to get help.

Otherwise, accept that you are not going to be good at everything, and that's okay.

I battled with feeling like a failed mother when my children were babies and toddlers. I couldn't seem to get organized and a trip to the mall was anticipated with great anxiety. I was so nervous I would forget something essential, that I invariably forgot something essential and would have to "wing it".

Friends tried to help me and acquaintances looked at me with disapproving condescension. I was depressed and refused to take medication for it, as I feared that would confirm that I was a bad mother.

Now my children are in elementary school, I am really enjoying the little people they are becoming. I am a good mother to this age bracket. We work things out together.

Some of this comes from my husband. For example, in our morning ritual, he makes the lunches. This simple act of help makes getting the family organized and out the door so much easier.

> For myself, I accept that I'm a "big picture" person and I need to put support in place where details are concerned.

Values

The values I hold dear are the ones Justin and I have emphasized to our children. Our role is to equip them for adulthood. We can teach them some things and we can draw on resources from others for support.

One of the values Justin and I work hard to instill in our children is the value of thinking for themselves. Being able to recognise peer and advertising pressure and more importantly, the motives behind it, will help them make better decisions. This requires a balance between teaching them to be unselfish team players (positive peer pressure can be motivating), whilst still encouraging individuality.

Some girls have been taught to "play nice" and be the peacemaker. This is another way of reinforcing giving in to those around us and puts us in danger of obeying the peer groups as we progress into teenager years and being 'used' as adults.

If we return to the analogy of the Warrior Princess, we can draw some parallels between the woman we want to be and the Princess we are inside.

The Warrior Princess

Let's imagine a modern princess.

Perhaps you'd prefer to see yourself as a Queen, and that's fine. I use the Princess example because she is in an ongoing process of development.

A princess does not wonder who she is; she knows where she belongs - ergo she is not threatened by the talents of others.

In fact, she seeks ways to enable them to make greater use of their talents because:

✓ It is good for them

✓ It benefits the Kingdom.

A Princess has the right to enjoy the benefits and liberties that are afforded to royalty.

A Princess also has responsibilities to her Kingdom. Her parents' job is to train her up so that over time she can take greater responsibility.

Who knows if and when Prince Charming will come along?

The Royal family has the responsibility of keeping the Kingdom in balance and prosperity. This is done through careful delegation.

She has been educated and the King is no fool so he utilizes her skills throughout the Kingdom.

Her basic military training has shown her where she needs to improve, in order to manage greater responsibility and authority.

She has learned to become a warrior for she understands that without this skill her country's enemies will eagerly step in and try to take the prosperity that has been so painstakingly created.

> She is extremely skilled with the double-edged sword because she practices regularly.

Humility

The Princess has sat at the feet of the elders listening to their wisdom. She is not too proud to ask questions. She knows their wisdom comes from good and bad experiences. Mistakes are to be shared and understood so wisdom and knowledge are preserved to ensure a better future. These are the lessons that teach her how to understand others.

The Princess must be discerning in order to recognise those suitable to be placed in senior positions, in middle management and so on.

> She recognizes the gifts of others and places them in positions in which they will flourish.

She does not have to imitate a prince because she knows her value is in who she is.

She does not need to bully those beneath her or assert her importance.

She respects the men of her Kingdom as individuals with gifts and talents. She commands respect from the men around her, not because she can swear as well as any of her troopers, but because her self-respect draws it from them.

She inspires them to more noble behavior and does not emasculate them. She sees their tendency to think differently as a benefit to the overall balanced running of the Kingdom.

She is a Warrior Princess.

Inside every woman is a warrior: inside every woman is a princess.

Look in the mirror, isn't she beautiful?

How you see yourself is not necessarily who you really are. You may not be the prettiest. You may not be the smartest. But understand Princess, you are worthy of respect. You may have to fight for it at times, but at others, you will elicit it without even trying.

Rise up daughter of the King for you truly are a Princess.

Life has given you some battles and certainly some battle scars. There will be times of tears and times of betrayal but no-one can rob you of your innate value.

Have courage in the face of adversity.

The battles are not over, but gird your loins, strengthen your arms, for there are others who need to be held and rocked and lifted up.

Girlfriend, if we don't do it for each other, who will?

A woman who values herself and others, is among the loveliest.

The Battle for the Minds of our Children

Our children are the targets of fraud long before they are directly approached. Once I had to explain to my daughter, who had only just learned to read, why a billboard is asking her if she wants longer lasting SEX.

Why do our little girls want to dress like scantily clad pop stars?

The sexualization of children in modern society is not helping our girls gain power. Nor is it helping them to understand what "self-respect" is.

Sexuality is an illusionary power. It brings short term gratification but lacks lasting value.

What do I mean by sexualization?

Our thoughts naturally gravitate to that which satisfies our flesh: gossip, other people's misery, other people's affairs, self-destruction and that which sexually stirs us.

The media is filled with images of teens in sexually provocative roles.

Why? Sex sells.

It's as simple as that. It's business. It's about defrauding a child of her innocence in order to make money. Companies farm younger fields to create new customers.

There was a time when society tried to protect children from adult concepts.

Sexual Role Models

A. The role model for a particular age group is the age group above it.

+ B. If our teens are obsessed with being skinny and looking sexy, our pre-teens naturally want to copy them.

+ C. Business is about supply and demand.

= D. Fashion becomes sexier at a younger age.

Unless we are proactive, our children are being preconditioned to be manipulated by someone else instead of making their own decisions.

Therese and I were young mums. While shopping together for children's underwear, at a leading department store, we came upon a wall of lingerie in sizes for 3 to 10-year-olds. They were tiny matching bra-lets and panties. They looked no different to the lingerie in the women's section except that the bras had flat cups.

Why would you dress a 6-year-old in a bra? Why a toddler? Is it really "cute"?

I reeled as I considered the pedophiles who would get excited at this clothing. Theresa had been defrauded of her innocence as a child and teenager. She became visibly upset, felt faint and had to leave the store.

Now we have 11-year-olds wearing things that are designed for older females who are trying to attract a mate.

Empowering your little Princess

It is up to us to educate our daughters (and sons). We need to instill in them the value of self-respect so they make healthy decisions, but such education takes both quality and quantity time.

My parents worked seven days a week around the time I hit puberty. I had been given "the sex talk", and shortly before puberty mum explained menstruation, provided me with the personal products I needed, and that was the end of it.

We never talked about boys and relationships and how to negotiate the pressures of being a teenager. She was also unaware that I was getting my moral values from romance novels (the juicier, the better).

Years later, I asked her why she'd never talked about morals and she said she just assumed I had the same ones as her!

It is so important to talk to your daughters about boys and relationships, even with their girl-friends.

Girls can be cruel and catty sometimes. We need to help them through these hurtful times as well. (Even when it's our girl who has been the nasty one!)

The only way we can do this is to make time for it.

Never underestimate the friendship of a father and daughter.

Dad can help her understand why boys are the way they are at certain ages.

Dad can also model what he would like his daughter to respond to in a boy.

When he models respect for her and her mother, she will come to expect that from a future mate. She will find disrespectful behavior unappealing.

My husband, Justin, individually takes our daughters on age-appropriate dates. He treats them like ladies and they can talk about anything they want to, even boys!

At a time when peer pressure is at its highest and life-changing decisions can be made in an instant, our daughters need to have the personal power of self-respect and independent, decision-making capabilities.

 Please don't be so busy that your daughter's peer group is left to tell her what "stage she should be up to" with a boy!

I urge you to empower your children to see the manipulation of advertising. You can help them intelligently assess the credibility of so-called media role-models and people of influence. Such a skill will serve them well when applied to a friend, partner, business opportunity or work colleague.

From a financial point of view, empowering children is not difficult. When my eldest daughter was three, we were at a pharmacy waiting on a prescription to be filled.

The pharmacy counter had wall-to-wall brightly colored packets of sweets which she wanted - now. I was able to explain that the shop was playing a game to try to trick us into parting with our money. The sweets are placed there deliberately to tempt us – but we would not be fooled!

"In fact if we can say 'no' often enough, we can use the accumulated money to buy a house, then another one. Before long we'll be able to afford all the sweets we want because we were able to say 'no' now!"

I had no problems with her nagging for sweets at shops after that.

Proactive Steps

Don't just buy things because your children desire them. Think about the influence of those purchases and indeed question where the desire for a particular product comes from.

 Slice through deception to get to the truth.

There is nothing sexually liberating about dressing preteens up in sexy clothes. If anything, it puts unnecessary pressure on them by drawing unwanted attention.

The opposite extreme is to cover up to the point where we are prisoners in our own garment.

When a woman has self-respect she doesn't have to prove anything.

A confident woman will elicit either respect or fear from a man, regardless of culture.

When it comes to viewing the promotional material of a business or a potential life-partner, the need for critical assessment is equally important.

Take the Warrior Princess Challenge...

1. Do you accept there are those who may envy you and those you will never please?

2. Do you agree it is not your job to please them?

3. Do you see your job is to be an effective leader?

4. Have you fallen for the belief that beauty is what is on the outside?

5. Do you practice kindness and exercise wisdom throughout your day? It helps promote that inner glow!

6. Are you willing to be responsible for your own continuing professional development?

7. Do you respect your subordinates as much as you desire or demand their respect?

Chapter Seven

Guarding Your Heart!

Guard your heart with all diligence, for out of it spring the issues of life."

Proverbs 4:23

At the risk of barbecuing a sacred cow, the issue of "gut-instinct" or "women's intuition" needs to be addressed because it is a heart issue.

While it is true that we get "feelings" about something or someone that sets up warning signals, we should not act on intuition alone.

 A healthy assessment of a situation comes from both subjective and objective research.

Having said that, instinct is often either put on a pedestal as some kind of spiritual guide or it is totally ignored.

I include Christians whose spirit is prompting them, too. Not all spirit promptings come from the Holy Spirit.

For some, it is mistaking "wishful thinking" for their "gut instinct". Still others are totally "by the numbers" and have become stone, motherless deaf to that inner prompting.

Neither approach is sound.

Distortions

Our gut-instinct can be distorted or blinded by our history.

My mother told me that I was very discerning as a child. There were those I would not go to, who later turned out to be less than honorable, and there were those I would warm to who were trustworthy. Nobody had to tell me.

Many children have this intuition.

Unfortunately, as I grew up and was taught "manners", I learned to ignore my inner warning signal. I had to accept those my parents accepted. A teenager showing her disapproval of an adult is not acceptable.

> Suspicion must be hidden lest it prompt rudeness.

Instinct Betrayed

An example of this is "Bubbles", a confident, loud, enormous man. I was about 13 and my parents owned a plant nursery. (To this day, my empathy runs deep for the child sitting on the side of the road selling flowers for Mother's Day; for I was she!)

Bubbles was always around as it was a seven-day business and he had partnered with my parents in a fountain centre to complement the nursery.

For some reason, I never took to him.

I found myself struggling not to be rude. He would take my hand and rub his big belly for "good-luck, just like Buddha". I wondered if my lack of warmth was jealousy of his time with my parents. It wasn't his bulk, because there were many large people in my life whom I loved.

I found him creepy and obnoxious but as the youth, I was the one required to respect the elder.

As it turned out he dealt fraudulently with my parents and disappeared. Ironically he was the first "born again" Christian we ever met; obviously the "wolf in sheep's clothing" kind. Fortunately, we were not so prejudiced that we thereafter labeled all "born-again" Christians as frauds.

Subtle Influences

When a child feels loved, cuddled, affirmed, respected and taught to respect others, he or she will grow up with a healthy self-esteem. They will naturally retain self-respect and respect of others.

If children only feel loved when they perform or when they are obedient, or when they are being touched inappropriately, their self-perception is way off kilter.

They will look at the world through distorted lenses and their expectations will be dictated by a learned love language.

 To constantly live with betrayal, cultivates untrusting or even untrustworthy adults.

It is their damaged spirit that betrays them. The damaged, violent spirit of a man is attracted to someone who will allow them to act out.

If his prey has been taught to obey without question, she will be unable to stand up for herself when she needs to.

A child who has been convinced that she is not worthy of respect, will, as an adult tolerate disrespectful behavior and even believe it is normal.

That is why the cycle continues. So often abused women connect with men who abuse them; they have subconsciously learned a pattern of behavior that attracts that type of man.

That is not to say it is the woman's fault, often they don't know it is happening.

If you have been brought up to be polite and accommodating, if your personality is to be a people pleaser, then be mindful that you will attract people who are happy to take advantage of your "niceness".

> You don't need to have been beaten up to have been abused.

Dirty Rotten Scoundrels

Earl Morris has protected the lives of Hollywood stars, diplomats and families all over the world. He is now using his knowledge and experience in assisting individuals and corporations to identify and diffuse potential violence. [www.lifeforceoneinternational.com.]

Earl teaches workshops on the prevention of child victimization and abuse. Earl is based on the Gold Coast, Australia and has much wisdom to offer when it comes to "uncovering dirty rotten scoundrels", in romance and finance.

For over 20 years Earl has made it his passion to protect people from violent human predators. This involves educating people and corporations about the warning signals of human predators and their processes.

> One thing he has learned over these years is that "a predator is a predator...is a predator!"

In his words: "those who prey upon others by manipulation, resulting in personal gain and gratification, are 'Human Predators'. Violence doesn't always have to play a role in this; sometimes it can be for financial gain!"

When it comes to security and safety, Earl believes soft or "politically correct" words to describe these predators, lessens our ability to realize the danger and peril. Not to mention the right actions to take to prevent or minimize them.

A victim of a crime is selected by the predator, it is not random!

The only aspect that may be random is how the predator came upon the potential victim, but make no mistake, the predator observed something from afar that assisted them in making the decision to select that person as their victim!

Earl also suggests that the main thing a predator looks for when selecting those they wish to "swindle", is vulnerability or perceived vulnerability. Vulnerability is easily spotted by a predator when they notice what Earl calls "Desperate Emotional Needs" (D.E.N.).

A 'D.E.N.' reveals itself as a passionate desire for connection or intimacy and a predator will take advantage of that, cultivating an environment for their scam to flourish. So how do I make myself less likely to be selected?

"First line of defense: Know thyself!"

Being aware of where your emotional vulnerabilities lie, will avoid them being exploited!

If you are openly passionate about the need for certain things in your life, like financial freedom, love or intimacy, be very protective of them and guard those areas carefully. They become your weak points when a predator is trying to gain your trust and friendship.

Developing sensitivity to people's intentions will also protect you from a master manipulator. If someone is trying to manipulate you with a view to fraud, there are signs or "pre-fraud" indicators and for the purpose of this book, I draw your attention to Earl's description of one of the primary human predators: seductive predators.

"Our ability to recognize a dangerous person or situation is programmed into every human being's nervous system."

The Seductive Predator

It is the seductive predator who is the "master at 'cloaking' their true motives and true directions. It's our 'early warning system' to danger that makes us safer...but we have to recognize it to take action!"

Everyone has come across people with whom they are not comfortable. It isn't easy to take them at face value. "I don't know, there is just something about him..."

Whether subconsciously or not, we recognize something isn't right when "what's coming out of a person's mouth doesn't match their physical behavior cues!"

Intuition

As mentioned previously, it is called many things, but that uneasy feeling we have about a person or situation is really Intuition. Not some mystical or New Age concept, but a very real and powerful ability possessed by all.

To quote Earl: "Intuition is the ability to unconsciously sense or know immediately without reasoning. We have seen CEO's, athletes, actors, soldiers etc. all comment about having a nagging feeling or a hunch about someone or something. Then, because of their acting on this, they avoided losing millions of dollars in shares, or turning down a particular movie role that would later have been disastrous either for their career or their very life."

Yet so often, we ignore that intuitive feeling.

Why?

"Denial" - Intuition's Adversary

Humans are motivated by two driving forces: "The Avoidance of Pain and The Seeking of Pleasure". The two sides to the coin!

Some choose denial when danger is staring them in the face because that is human nature.

Our nervous systems are hard-wired to seek out that which would bring us the most pleasure or to do whatever we can to avoid pain. Our brains will work overtime to create ways of avoiding anything painful, such as confronting a lover who we fear is cheating on us or trying to swindle us. Our brain is really partial to denial and uses it frequently. It is in our nature to deny what is obvious in order to avoid unpleasant experiences.

Predators know all about denial and avoidance.

There are many signals, if you are looking, that indicate if a stranger or new person in your life is trying to manipulate you to "their way of thinking", or to gain your trust.

Only with this trust can they get you to give them what they want without resorting to threats, coercion or violence.

Read through the following signals of manipulation and if you can, think back to a time you had to deal with a sales person, like buying a house or car etc...you may recognize three or more of these signals when they were trying to sell you something.

Earl's Signals of Manipulation

Semi-insulting Labeling – Trying to get you to disprove!

"You're probably the type of woman who is suspicious of every man huh?" Here they know that this is not true but they know most people will go out of their way to aggressively disprove this theory of themselves. We all want to be liked and they know this.

You Scratch My Back – Trying to get you in their debt!

When you think back to when you were a child and you owed a favor to a friend, and how hard it was to say "no" when they wanted something else in return.

Promises by a Stranger – Used to convince people to place their faith in the person!

Ask yourself if confronted by this: "Why does this stranger want to convince me?" It is made by the stranger to offset doubts displayed by your facial or body language.

Not taking "NO" for An Answer – Discounting the word "NO" means trying to control you!

When someone doesn't take no for an answer, you should ask yourself: "Why is this person trying to control me?" They know that most woman don't want to appear to be a "B.I.T.C.H." so they will keep pushing until you draw the line in the sand!

(Oh, by the way ladies, always remember B.I.T.C.H. for me and for you should stand for Boys I'm Taking Charge Here!!)

Forced Partnership – Trying to force commonality between you and them!

"We're in the same boat together" attitude.

Charm – Is a skill and not an inherent trait of a person! Just like building rapport with someone, charm always has a motive!

Niceness does not always equal goodness! While it can sometimes be a personality trait, it is not necessarily the true nature of a person.

Too Many Details – Who are they trying to convince... themselves?

This can be seen with anyone trying to deceive or conceal the truth. The person doing the lying has an internal conflict going on because they know they are lying. (This applies to "non-pathological" liars.)

Many times people give too many details when lying because they are trying to unconsciously convince themselves and, in turn, convince their intended victim.

Clusters

Individually, these signals aren't synonymous with something bad. We all use them in our lives to develop relationships and connections with others. They are ways of establishing trust. However, be wary if you are experiencing a cluster of these signals from the one person. One or two doesn't mean you are a target, but if three or more, listen to the ringing warning bells in your inner woman.

 Remember to participate in your own rescue.

Romantic Boundaries

As you get to know someone of the opposite sex, there is usually a point when you decide that you would like to be a closer friend.

Then at some point in that friendship you may toy with the idea of a romance. When you feel yourself starting to be attracted to someone and you fall into your pattern of flirting, learn from your history and recall where it normally leads.

It's best to decide what your boundaries will be before you get into a romantic situation.

It's at the point where you are considering taking the friendship to the next level that you need to do some serious due-diligence. You have a small window of opportunity to assess, investigate, and try to make a rational decision. Use it wisely.

There are many good men who have a dark past. Not one of us has a perfect background. I don't suggest you write them off, just be aware of what you are getting into and the potential risks. You don't need a license, or to pass a test to have sex. Passion can cause rash decisions.

Having one wonderful night does not mean that moving in together will make every night wonderful.

Remember, each relationship we enter into will leave its mark on our children's hearts as well.

Don't remain naïve, it's too risky.

Begin investigating their suitability as a mate, even if you really only want a light romance. While you are asking your girlfriends what they know about him and what kind of money he earns, ask yourself some revealing questions. Be brave enough to accept the answers. Although no guarantee, heartache may be avoided.

The pain of regret is far greater than the pain of self-discipline.

If you create criteria just as you would a set of KPIs for a prospective employee, (or use the KPIs for Romance provided) you will minimize risk to yourself and your family.

KPIs for Romance:

✓ Has he ever had a different last name?

✓ Does he have comprehensive insurance?

✓ Does he have a criminal past?

✓ Has he been accused of anything?

✓ What do his previous partners say about him?

✓ What does he say about them?

✓ What moral values would you like him to have?

✓ How does he handle temptation?

✓ Is saving money for the future important to him?

✓ What kind of education does he value?

✓ Is he well mannered or is he brutish?

Take the Princess Warrior Challenge...

- Identify things you are passionate about.

- Know them well; they could easily be your areas of vulnerability.

- Make a list of possible D.E.N.s that could be targeted by a predator.

- Have there been times in the past when you know your intuition stepped in and saved you from making a poor decision?

- Do you listen to your intuition? Do you have confidence in your intuition?

- Is Denial something you struggle with?

- Have your ever used denial to avoid confrontational situations?

- Look for signals of manipulation over the next week or so. Do you recognise them in yourself?

- Do you easily recognise them in others?

Chapter Eight

Warning Signals...

Business and Romantic

This chapter looks at crossing the line between romantic and business fraud.

We are learning that warning signals are always there, but we don't always notice them.

Hindsight provides 20/20 vision. Often people will remark that they made the best decision they could at the time with the information they had.

That would be true on the surface; however, our subconscious desires, or simple laziness, can prevent us from looking deeper. The information on which we base our decision could possibly be better interpreted.

Unsolicited Approach

Jane, a pastry chef, received a call from an old school chum she had not seen in 15 years. Jason had been in touch with mutual friends and discovered that she was newly single. He was too.

Would she like to catch up for coffee? He was new to a finance company and would really appreciate the opportunity to "practice his spiel" on her. No pressure to buy.

He wanted to practice on someone he knew, but not well, so it would feel like a stranger without being too scary. He really needed to make the job work as he was supporting two young boys.

Jane felt sorry for him and agreed.

What she didn't know was that Jason had found out from the mutual friends that Jane's divorce had resulted in her being left with a number of assets she didn't know what to do with.

Jason used reverse psychology and at the same time, regularly referred to her need for security and to look for a company that cared about her interests.

> The practice session was a ploy to create a false sense of trust in Jason.

Jason emphasized that he was not trying to sell her anything. He did not want to appear to be taking advantage of their friendship.

In fact, he had been badly hurt by abuse as a boy and found it hard to confide in people. He understood what it felt like to be betrayed as Jane had been in the past.

This only made Jane trust him more as he seemed to have her interests at heart.

He also practiced a chivalry that his ex-wife had never seen. He talked about wanting his children to grow up secure and how happy he was to be with his new company.

> Jane began to feel a measure of attraction for Jason.

She hadn't been treated so well by a man in a while.

Jane was hooked.

The papers all seemed a bit complex so she just signed them after Jason explained them verbally to her. Assets were realized and money was transferred all under her kind friend's considerate gaze.

Then he did not return her calls. In fact, the company told her he had left their employ but under the privacy act, could not give her any details.

As for her investment, there was no record of her money going into their company account. The account Jason had set up was in another company name and had since been closed, the money wired overseas.

Hindsight lesson #1

Think about how you are known by this person. Work out what they already know about you and where they could have obtained that information.

Hindsight lesson #2

Don't reveal your assets and your fears too early. In business or in romance, you want them to be interested in your company or you, first.

Also be wary if they boast too much about their own success. It is normal for a bloke to try to impress a girl with his assets, but not if he talks about his success at length.

At best, it is bad manners and boorish [perhaps they are over-compensating other inadequacies]. At worst, he is trying to deceive you.

Common Traits:

If someone has infiltrated your club or church for example, he will speak and dress like those who are members. His goal is to win the trust of those around him, then try to do business with them.

Sometimes he may even begin a romance with a mature single lady with assets and influence, in order to reach and fleece others.

In the movie, "Sleepless in Seattle", the comment is made that a single woman in her 40s has more chance of being killed by a terrorist than finding a man.

Meg Ryan's character quickly retorted, "That's not true!"

Her single friend Becky laments, "I know, but it feels true!"

The deal is not stacked in a woman's favor if she feels lucky just to get a man's attention.

 It can be tempting to not look too closely for fear of discovering something unacceptable.

Just as a good sales assistant has been trained in how to "read" you, to a con-artist, the lonely and vulnerable are like a well-read book.

The con-artist has usually studied body language in order to more effectively manipulate his prey; however there can still be certain "tells" that give him away.

They might have a twitch when sharing important information. They may be trying too hard to keep looking you in the eye. Body language books such as those of Alan Pease are fascinating. They will certainly help you read people better and also help you hide your own "tells" when assessing an opportunity or a purchase.

Just remember, a good con has read Alan's books too, and will have been practicing... For instance, a person folding his arms might be cold. If they are folding their arms, crossing their legs and leaning away from you, it's a cluster of signals indicating that they probably would prefer to be somewhere else. Remember, warning signals come in clusters as Earl pointed out and the following is a list, not exhaustive by any means.

It's a mix of business, romantic and spiritual characteristics that I have noticed over the last twenty years.

Warning Signals to Watch Out For:

- A disdain for traditional ways of doing business or investing. It's one thing to be an individual, an entrepreneur, the next Richard Branson. It's quite another to manipulate the law and try to assure a person that what they are doing is "Not illegal!"

- If a person feels the need to assure you of a scheme's legality, tell them you will want to run it past your lawyer, or ask to speak to the lawyer who advised them.

- Often they will talk about how the government does not really want ordinary people to become wealthy and why there are so many restrictions placed on investment.

- They will talk about the global market and how clever it is to have off-shore accounts and tax-havens. (There is nothing wrong with investing off-shore, just be sure the particular investment is legal and what recourse you may have if it goes bad.)

- They will sometimes talk about the constitution and how technically, you should not have to pay tax.

- A sense that "The Establishment" does not understand big dreamers. After all, great achievers were never understood during their struggle. They will trot out the Colonel Sanders story of how he went to so many banks before he found one that would back him. They refer to Edison's statement that he'd found 999 ways that a light bulb will not work. They utilize all the illustrations motivational speakers use in order to get you believing what a logical, conservative person would not.

- They claim to be self-taught in their giftedness with their business and they get extraordinary returns because they did not learn what "the rest" learned. For example, currency trading.

103

- They are masters at making conspiracy theories sound plausible. Ordinary people will have ordinary lives, but they have found a way to succeed that few will find out about. You are worthy of this information!

- One of their conspiracy theories might be about how we should not have to pay tax. It will go back to some obscure old document that wasn't ratified properly etc. Or perhaps the idea that because we are sons of God and God owns the Earth, the son does not need to pay tax. Governments are the invention of Man. (Women don't usually play a role of significance for these people apart from their usefulness for serving cakes and tea at their get-togethers.) Women are not usually granted any authority in their organization either.

- Often their view of sex is either very repressive or very permissive. There is little middle ground. Depending on how much influence they have over you already, you may be persuaded to compromise your values because of your attraction.

- A disdain for certain aspects of religious life, especially any reference to giving money. They claim to be generous, but often are critical of ministers who talk about offerings or "tithing".

- Those who protest too much about giving finance are often just using religious talk to justify being stingy.

- A professed, devoted, believer who speaks disdainfully of other believers.

- Overly charismatic. There is often a little fan club that agrees with everything he says, giving him "guru" status.

- He may chide you, saying that your disagreeing with him is the result of your past "issues". Your problem with their way of doing things is a problem you have with "authority".

- Inconsistencies about his past. These may not come up until well into the relationship.

- Asserting that he is not interested in taking you for a ride (Why the need to say so?).

- He may create "trust tests" to make you think he is trustworthy. This could mean pretending to find someone's wallet and emphasizing that the money was still in it. Ostentatious displays designed to sweep you off your feet are under the category of "too good to be true".

The "Super-Spirro"

Over the years I've experienced people who are spiritually "too good to be true". This means they are so spiritual that you cannot have a normal conversation with them. It's as if they have to prove themselves. They often begin sentences with "God told me this" or "God told me that".

I don't have a problem with someone believing God has spoken to them. Indeed I have felt God speak softly to my spirit at times. The issue of credibility comes when it's used for selfish or manipulative purposes. It might also be that they go on and on and on about why scripture supports their little "soapbox".

It is normal to be passionate about something that has changed your life. To a non-spiritual person, someone who attends church any more than they do is weird.

A new convert may rabbit on about their new love for Christ until he temporarily drives his friends crazy. That doesn't make him or her suspect. A seemingly super-spiritual person may be just very passionate about the spiritual experience they have had or they can be hiding their real selves from you.

As a pastor, my father has ministered healing to many victims of child abuse and sometimes even the perpetrators.

Perpetrators overcompensate by appearing overly spiritual, often obsessed with their perceived "authority".

Super-spirituality, the kind where you cannot have a "normal" conversation, is often a smoke-screen to prevent them revealing their real selves. It can sometimes be a sign of a hidden lust problem. Or it might be that they desire to present themselves as some kind of spiritual leader. They often have strong opinions about obscure historical facts and ancient writings.

This over-compensation usually masks low self-esteem issues.

Bill was a very passionate man who loved to talk about the end of the world. He invited me to join him in his cave in Israel where he was storing tinned food to sustain us when Armageddon came.

I was about 18 at the time and was not particularly impressed with the idea of the world ending before I'd met my husband! "What about everybody else?" I asked. "Your plan sounds a bit selfish to me. Good luck though – and don't forget your can-opener!"

Ay Caramba!

I met a businessman who claimed to love God and held bible studies in his office. However, when he came to church as our guest, he sat at the back as he was uncomfortable being in the third row with us, his hosts!

Again, notice the small cluster. It wasn't where he sat, it was the fact that as a guest he didn't want to sit with his hosts and the front area made him uncomfortable. Yet he claimed to hear from God.

As it turned out, he was an undischarged bankrupt seeking investment money from the nice, church people to fend off the puppet directors he'd put in place who were trying to steal the business he had no legal right to be running! It's the classic case of "If I can't be the leader, I don't want to play."

Beware of that self-important attitude in business as well as life. It reminds me of reincarnation stories where rarely has anyone been a normal person in a previous boring life. Their previous lives are usually that of a Princess or a slave or something exciting. Hmmm.

If you are spiritual, it is important that you are spiritually compatible. If however, it seems like there is nothing but spirituality to a man, you have to ask if he is being real. Is he just trying to impress you or is he trying to avoid talking about how he really feels?

At the same time, a truly spiritual person bears fruit. They don't need to dress like a swami; they just demonstrate their sincerity with action and character.

> Nobody is perfect, but a truly spiritual person is humble and considerate of others.

It is as unrealistic for a man to go on "ad nauseum" about spiritual matters, as it is for him to continue to shower you with flowers and gifts, unless it is particular to his character.

Some men will shower you with gifts in order to stop you talking about things that bother you. "How can I confront him now when he has done this for me? I'm so ungrateful..."

While we dream of finding a man to fulfill our every fantasy, I will repeat the obvious: nobody is perfect. Chances are if he is perfect, then you would not be compatible anyway!

Questions for Business Opportunities and Romance:

- What are my motives for this deal or relationship?

- Does the deal stack up fairly?

- What impact will it have on my personal life and on my family if it doesn't work out?

- What is the worst case scenario?

- What am I prepared to lose?

- What else could I lose that I haven't thought of e.g. reputation?

- Have I sought advice from a professional?

- Am I willing to seek advice from a "devil's advocate"?

- Am I avoiding those who would discourage me?

- Do I quickly label those who would discourage me from the venture as "negative"?

- Are my heart and my head arguing?

- Am I justifying peculiarities?

- What am I putting at risk e.g. children, privacy etc?

- Can you walk away from the deal?

- Am I afraid to ask for personal information or financials?

Chapter Nine

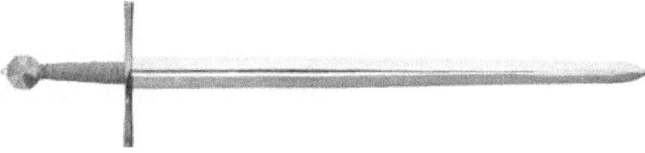

Sharpening Your Sword...
Due-diligence of the Heart

Our heart is like a garden. From the time we are little, it is tended in some way. Some gardens are tended lovingly and carefully, others are neglected either in parts, or totally. Still others have become rubbish dumps that uncaring people have trashed.

If a part of our garden has been trashed, we will usually do one of two things:

1. Put a barbed wire fence around that part so nobody can add to it.

2. Agree that that spot is a rubbish dump and allow more people to trash it.

Our garden sets the scene and provides the presuppositions by which we make judgments about people. Would you purchase a property without having a building and pest report done?

Of course not!

Then why on earth would you not check their background before allowing a person to move into your heart, your home, your wallet, your bed and your family?

Maybe it is because approval comes from the garden of our heart and this person makes us feel good. In a harsh, lonely world it's natural to want more of what makes us feel good.

How can our children expect to grow up to have healthy, drug-free, faithful relationships when they grow up on a steady diet of soap operas, worshiping celebrities and sporting figures of questionable character?

But...It's not all doom and gloom...there are good men out there. Honest, reliable, hard-working men who love kids and are generous, kind, intelligent and sensitive without being gay (Okay, I'm going out on a limb with that last one!).

Just don't expect it all in the one package!

> If you are looking for Mr. Perfect, consider whether you are Mrs. Perfect material.

The Knight in Shining Armor…

One day their Prince came...and went...so they found another one...who came and went...then there were none left...

And people ask why depression in women is at an all time high? Our romantic hopes are repeatedly squashed by reality. What makes it so easy for romantic frauds to take advantage of successful women?

Inside women, there beats a desire for the knight in shining armor to gallop up and sweep us off our feet to live happily ever after...

Unfortunately many decent, trustworthy blokes don't even know how to ride, let alone perform tricks!

In the "dog-eat-dog" business world, if a man shows old fashioned gallantry, good manners, refrains from swearing in front of ladies and even comes to your aid in times of trouble, he can easily become the knight in shining armor that, as a girl, you went to sleep dreaming of.

Our instincts respond to our deep desire to find that special kind of man, one "not like the rest", who will cherish us, like we deserve. In

110

a culture focused on self-gratification, materialism and economic prosperity – kindness and thoughtfulness stand out like beacons.

Sometimes the knight is a genuine good guy, but sometimes, ah well...

A gentleman scammer will perform that role until we are so caught up that even if our instinct tries to warn us, it's too late. Sometimes these romantic strategies are used to simply get sex. You are the goal that is scored and interest is quickly lost.

Sometimes the motive is more sinister. Appearing honorable will encourage someone to think a person is also honest. Women in their forties and above are particularly vulnerable to the "gentlemanly" approach.

A scammer's strategy can include appearing more "open and honest" than normal. For example they may say "I've never told anyone this, but I was badly abused as a child." Maybe they were and maybe it's a line to bring out your nurturing side. Even if it were true, while it's sad he was abused, it doesn't mean he is a good person.

It does mean he will have baggage you will need to deal with at some point if he hasn't had help getting over it.

Your own baggage will only exacerbate problems if your past has not been dealt with.

Let's face it. There are few children of the 70s and 80s whose parents did not break-up. How many "uncles" and "aunties" have traversed through the lives of children and teens, providing questionable role modeling?

I'm grateful that I grew up with a wonderful step-father. Don't feel guilty about creating a blended family. Just consider the blend carefully before mixing. A child that has had an emotionally unhealthy childhood is vulnerable to manipulation of the heart as an adult.

111

When your self-esteem is healthy, you can look more objectively at what is coming towards you.

Guarding your heart and keeping your sword sharp will, in fact, prepare you to recognise when someone worthy does arrive on the scene. While you are wasting years of your life waiting for your gambling addicted boyfriend to change, husband material could be passing right by you.

Sometimes the decent ones can take a little longer to mature, but then, we ladies can take a while to "wake up" too. In our "modern" society, why are we so shocked when a partner cheats if they have a history of promiscuity before the relationship?

Even people who are not married are devastated when their partner turns to someone else. Why?

I do not recommend promiscuity but consider the following: If we are supposed to be primates, why do we expect our partner or even ourselves, to remain faithful when primates don't?

There are those who would argue that on the basis of "nature", fidelity is "unnatural"!

In spite of the prevalence of adultery, most people cling to the idea of fidelity as being something they are entitled to. Why?

The answers to all these questions lie in the heart.

We are not monkeys - We are human beings.

We have an innate consciousness of right and wrong - animals do not.

There is something in us that desires intimacy and exclusivity. We desire something noble and true and honest.

Everyone is at different stages of reaching out. Some have become dysfunctional in their efforts but all look for fulfillment. The romantic fraud knows this only too well. That is what he or she plays on.

When we know our areas of vulnerability we can protect them.

It's important to start with knowing who you are and that you are worthy of respect. Respect others and respect yourself.

Practice on yourself by having a little talk with yourself about the way you handle your emotions.

> No matter how much abuse we've suffered, everyone wants to be loved.

Due-diligence on Ourselves:

What is it that you want in a partner?

First make a list - a realistic one.

Then write out a second list of the characteristics you think he would want in a partner. Be totally honest.

Do you fit that description?

Now, answer these next questions with the same honesty:

What are the insecurities you've carried from your past?

If you were abused, have you recovered? How do you know?

Do you need counseling? If so get some.

Do you have any unreasonable pet hates? Where did they come from?

Can you reframe your hang-ups in a helpful light?

Sometimes learning some NLP techniques can help. Neuro-Linguistic Programming can help you to see your experiences in a less destructive light.

Do you fly off the handle?

When you feel anger start to rise, try this little exercise - run to another room if possible and go through this self-examination. Why am I angry? What was said that triggered it?

Was there any truth in it?

Do you believe YOU are valuable?

Whatever your religious beliefs, if any, you need to believe that you are valuable just as you are, not for what you contribute.

My natural father is now my friend. However, as a younger man, alcohol got the better of him and ruined a number of marriages.

Broken relationships can often produce boys who are emotionally distant and girls who are emotionally clingy. When these two try to create a life together, they are behind the eight-ball to start with.

I had suffered rejection and fear as a child. As a teenager, I wanted a boyfriend because I believed that would make me feel pretty and important and give me popularity. Not terribly good reasons.

I had grown up on a steady diet of Mills and Boon romance novels. I didn't get involved with many boys because I lacked confidence.

Finally my prince charming came on the scene. The only problem was that he didn't know his lines! He had not read the same romance novels as I had.

Once I was married I struggled for some years to believe that my husband really loved me. I was emotionally clingy and had unrealistic expectations of my husband early in our marriage. My low self-esteem drove me to test him and seek reassurance and fulfillment from him. Of course this was asking too much.

He grew up in a sporting family who did not like to talk about emotions, nor were they physically demonstrative. I did very little due-diligence. I knew he was a good catch because he was handsome, well-mannered, had a job and a pulse!

Fortunately, we shared the same values and morals so our difficulties were overcome with a lot of prayer and personal development, mostly on my part!

It was not until I accepted who I was that I found my significance and value as a human being.

I am a daughter of God who made me and loves me as I am.

Romantic Due-diligence:

Most people's idea of romantic due-diligence is to jump in the sack to find out if they are "compatible".

Some of the best romantic due-diligence a person can do is to spend time with a potential partner's family. If possible do it before you become romantic as they are likely to be more themselves if you are still just a friend.

Foolishness cannot be legislated against.

My mum always said:

"Watch how he treats his mother, that's how he'll treat you!"

She also said, "Never lend your car or your boyfriend because neither will come back quite the same!"

Wise woman, my mum.

My step-Dad was always a man of few words. The classic strong silent type, a gentle giant that kids adored, including me. I got to know him as a friend only after I'd started university and realized the world was not all about me and my opinions!

I also wanted to understand men better as I was on the look-out for Mr. Right.

Dad's single pearl of wisdom was a very politically incorrect generalization, born from years of life experience as a man, including two decades as a pastor:

> "Whatever a man is, marriage will make him more so. An angry man will become a violent man."

We are vulnerable when we do not know how to guard ourselves. It's a good idea to put you and your prospective partner in situations where there is pressure, for example:

- Volunteer for a convention of some kind where you have to be organized, give customer service and work hard together.

- How about helping on a retreat for difficult children? They can really test attitudes.

The following list offers relevant questions that may assist you in discovering some of his pressure points. It wouldn't hurt to ask yourself these questions as well.

- Ask him about his worst experiences in business and in life. How did he handle it? Does he still bubble with anger at the thought of it? What went wrong? Whose fault was it? This will show whether he can take responsibility for his decisions.

- Is there anyone he currently blames or hates? What are his reasons?

- If necessary, would you both be willing to go to a pre-appointed mediator if just one of you thinks it is important?

- Do you know how he supports his current lifestyle?

- What are his other fiscal responsibilities e.g. ex-spouse, kids?

- How does he feel about having to pay child support?

- How do you feel about him having these commitments? They will affect your lifestyle with him.

- How well does he budget? What are his budgeting priorities? Is he a saver or is he just stingy? What about you?

- Is he a giver? How do you feel about that?

- Is he foolishly generous or are you the stingy one?

One of my priorities has always been to tithe. That means to give away at least 10% of my income. If Justin had not been in agreement with that philosophy, I would not have dated him.

He disagrees as he is sure his overwhelming charm would have won me over! However, part of my attraction to him was his kind heart and generosity. When I saw the photo of a sponsor child in his bachelor flat, I decided he was one of the good guys. How many single young blokes do that?

(It is true that a fraudster could have a number of photos of "sponsor children" that he is not really sponsoring, so I admit I took a risk.)

If in doubt, tactfully ask for proof of their giving and don't feel guilty for asking. A classic example is the ring that has been "in the family for generations". Fraudsters will spin the story, hoping you won't notice they didn't outlay a cent.

Any giving they do is considered an investment. In other words, part of the sting!

117

Are you a Baggage Handler?

With so many relationships beginning between people in their forties, it is to be expected that there will be "baggage". Even if you only plan to live together, it is sensible to do some thorough due-diligence prior to the commitment.

In many instances abuse of children is perpetrated by "mum's boyfriend". It may not be romantic to carry out a background check, but surely your children are worth the effort?

It's normal to ask his family and friends about him early on. You would like to hear stories of his childhood, past girlfriends and wives, etc. Getting a background check is just an extension of what you would do anyway.

The services of a private detective can provide a background check that reveals inconsistencies in his story and even potential danger. A background check can reveal bankruptcy, court action, suspect relationships, adultery etc.

If he has a problem with your curiosity, consider it a warning signal and find out why.

Short-listing the Candidate

It doesn't hurt for you to ask him about his past in case you encounter some "awkward" moments in your future.

I don't believe a person needs to disclose their past sins, however, if there is an area of vulnerability and you are **aware** of it, and then you are more able to support and protect him.

If he is addicted to pornography, you need to decide whether this is something he must overcome with your help, or if you don't mind.

Before you decide that you don't mind, research the effects of an addiction to pornography...you might change your mind. If you still decide you don't mind, then make yourself fully aware of the risks.

A life that is dominated by sexual images can make a person vulnerable to cheating.

Beware of being too accepting just because society says it's okay, or because you had an upbringing that was the opposite and you swore you'd never be as narrow minded as your parents.

The following are just a few questions that you should find answers for, before you make that big commitment:

- Is he good with children? Do children like him?

- Do you have similar views on how to raise them?

- When around his own children, how does he talk about their mother, his ex?

- If there have been drink driving charges, you will need to consider whether that could happen again.

- Is your time together characterized by binge drinking?

- If you met over an ecstasy tablet, well, good luck because you are asking for trouble.

- If you customarily require a couple of wines each night, test yourself with a different routine to make sure you have not created an unhealthy dependence. Can he go without alcohol in a situation where he normally would drink?

- Does he change when he is around his buddies?

- What are their girlfriends/partners/wives like?

- How are they treated by their men?

- Does he ignore you when around work colleagues?

- Is he surly around your work colleagues?

- Does he try to keep you away from your family?

- Does he resent your girlfriends or your career?

- Is he gay or just well dressed and articulate?

Guard your heart with all diligence for out of it flow the issues of life.

Proverbs 4:23

Take the Princess Warrior Challenge

- What expectations were planted in the garden of your heart?

- Do you have a healthy friendship (i.e. the nonsexual part of the relationship)?

- How does he treat his mother? (potential issues with you)

- Does he respect his father? (potential issues with authority)

- What do you really know about his history and background?

- What therapy has he had and how does he know if it helped?

Chapter Ten

Sharpening Your Sword...

Due-diligence in Business

"Too often we enjoy the comfort of opinion without the discomfort of thought."　　　　　John F. Kennedy

There are three areas that require due-diligence when it comes to a business deal:

1. The deal
2. The person or people with whom you will deal
3. Yourself

Any one of these three areas can let you down.

The Deal

Do the numbers stack up?

What needs to happen for the numbers to work?

Who prepared the numbers?

Was it an accountant?

How accountable are they? In other words are the numbers predicated on ideal market conditions?

How might adverse, natural conditions affect the project and is there a contingency plan? For example, what effect might a drought have on the project? It could affect production or it could affect demand.

I once invested in a project involving harvesting the plasma in the blood of cattle.

Cattle were kept on a farm and some of their blood was taken periodically. The blood was sold to companies that made use of the by-products.

These companies preferred the high quality blood from our cattle because of the controlled environment that kept the cattle healthy. Otherwise, they would have to purchase blood from an abattoir where blood is plentiful but not as great a priority for quality control as the meat.

The investment went well until eventually the drought which had dogged Australia for years finally had an effect on the cost of upkeep and the investment ended.

 In order to attract capital, developers and brokers will talk about a project being underway when it hasn't yet begun.

Can You Visit the Project Site?

Carol was being asked to invest in a building project that apparently had approval for 37 townhouses in an area of high demand. She wisely asked Barry, a friend who had sold real estate for 3 0 years to come along to the meeting to help her ask the right questions about the project.

Vince was very excited about the fact that he had been awarded the project and was eagerly talking about the professionals who were involved.

Barry asked, "How many of the 37 townhouses have begun construction?"

"Three," replied Vince proudly.

"Great," said Barry. "Where is the closest one we can visit?"

"Oh, er, actually, it could be a bit, um. You know I'll have to talk to the foreman and get back to you, there are, um, workplace health and safety issues and, er, a confidentiality agreement to organize and, well, I'll get back to you on that one."

Hedging and stalling are common practices when a person is speaking of the potential of a project as though it's already done.

Options to Buy

Another case in point is the business of options. Normally options refer to shares. You pay a small premium for the right to purchase a share at a preset price within a given time, regardless of the actual price at the time you want to actually make the purchase.

In recent years options to purchase have become popular with property buyers.

Michael and Kate thought they were doing a joint venture with their financial advisor on a sub-dividable property in a booming coastal town. Since their advisor was also their accountant, they left him to organize the deal and simply deposited their funds into his company trust account and received an appropriate certificate of deposit.

Instead of paying the deposit on the property, the advisor used their money to pay for a 12 month "option to buy" premium on the development. It seems he had many of these "deals" with other clients and expected to make sufficient money to be able to revisit and complete the purchase before the option ran out and all would be well.

Unfortunately, the option did run out and the money was lost. Michael and Kate only found out about the lies from the appointed liquidator.

The Person

Sometimes a person in a place of special trust, such as a financial advisor or accountant, can become overconfident in their ability. In this case, the man was extremely intelligent and apparently felt that the end justified the means, and what Michael and Kate didn't know wouldn't hurt them.

Beware of people who seem "cleverer" than everyone else in their industry. Beware of not having sufficient accountability strategies in place.

"Power corrupts and Absolute Power corrupts absolutely!"

When dealing with anyone who has any kind of authority or expertise, be very careful to separate their authority from their accountability. This applies to all situations even when dealing with someone who is normally your supervisor, religious overseer, leader in a club or head of a committee.

It can be difficult for some people with any kind of expertise or authority in one area of your life, to switch that off and see you as an equal or even submit to your expertise in other areas.

Doing so takes humility, so beware of those who are in danger of believing their own press!

The most expensive lawyer is not always the best.

For more detailed advice on assessing deals, I recommend Hans Jakobi's book Due-diligence Made Simple. If you are going to invest a significant amount of money, consider hiring a professional investigator to find out things that normal due-diligence will not reveal.

It's amazing what you can find out.

I met Michael Featherstone of Phoenix Global in May, 2007. He is a corporate and private investigator with 3 decades of experience. He was presenting at a business breakfast on the subject of how to Bullet Proof Your Business.

I asked him a simple question: "Have you ever heard of xxxx xxxx?"

"I sure have, he's a mate of a Sydney underworld figure. How do you know him?"

Needless to say, if I'd been able to have that two-line conversation at the point of considering an investment, I would have saved myself a lot of grief.

I got to know Michael and became very impressed with his operation, to the point where I insisted he should have someone promoting his services.

I became that person. Phoenix Global is both my client and one of my resources for my business talks.

In the process I discovered that small business is extremely vulnerable to fraud because of a simple dangerous mindset. The classic "It won't happen to me!" This leads to the third area requiring due-diligence:

Yourself!

Entrepreneurs are risk-takers by nature. Unfortunately their great strength is also their great weakness. We can be so gung-ho about a deal that we are tempted to take shortcuts or overestimate our own business acumen.

This is especially true when we've had some success.

The fact is that a little knowledge can be worse than none!

When you do not expect to fail, other people's failures are not relevant to you.

125

James and Julie were working on their third renovation. They had made good money on the first two and were excitedly encouraging their friends to do the same.

They were so buoyed by their success that they were considering starting a business helping other people renovate.

They had a rethink when their latest renovation produced new and more expensive problems; consequently they became more circumspect in their advice.

Youthful hubris need not only apply to age, but also experience.

An excellent book on this area is The E-Myth Revisited by Michael Gerber. It explores how each of us wears one of three hats:

1. Technician
2. Manager
3. Entrepreneur

When you know what you are best at you can protect your weaker areas by getting training or by delegating.

 It is important to know your business self. Just as with romance, you need to know your own areas of vulnerability, you also need to know your areas of weakness.

Delegating or Dumping again?

As a legacy from our school days, where report cards urged us to improve our low marks, we often try to improve our weaknesses in business at the expense of our strengths. The idea should be to become balanced and gradually improve overall.

A more recent business theory is that we should give free reign to our strengths and delegate our weaknesses.

This is a very exciting concept but one which also requires deeper self-assessment, for it is tempting to ignore important areas of responsibility because you just can't get excited about it.

Even if you are not "good" with the accounts, you still have a responsibility to know what is going on.

According to Bob Harrison of Increase ministries:

> "People will not do what is expected. They will only do what is inspected!"

The following successful woman has been appointed a member of the Order of Australia (AM) by Queen Elizabeth II. She received this honor for her services to the community, in particular in the area of women's issues.

Lynette Palmen AM is an entrepreneur who established Women's Network Australia in 1990. Inspired by her own personal and business experiences in the corporate sector during the Eighties and Nineties, she set out to design an organization based on what she wished had been available to her.

I value Lynette's experience and wisdom and asked her to share some of it:

"In my role for the past 20 years as the Managing Director of Women's Network Australia, I have met thousands of women in business.

For those whose businesses have gone bust they most certainly always have a tale of woe about the fact they thought someone was keeping an eye on cash flow, stock or whatever and when it came down to it this person was not holding up their side of the bargain.

The lesson to be learnt here is that you cannot expect anyone or trust anyone to oversee your business; especially the finances of your business, as well as you would do it yourself.

As large as WNA has become, I authorize and pay all the accounts personally and control and complete cash flow 130 and projections for the company. Naturally I seek guidance and expertise from accountants etc., but I do not hand the responsibility to anyone else and never will, regardless of how large the company becomes.

My tip here is to always retain this job and seek assistance with other areas of less overall importance to the business.

Unfortunately, too many business owners hand over the financial management, preferring to concentrate on the more creative areas of their business.

Like most things in life, it is about balance. Not everything in your career or business will make your heart flutter. Some aspects are not as glamorous as others.

I say whatever keeps you awake at night needs your attention and personally I would rather it be a good man than poor cash flow or my business failing!"

Amen to that, sister!

In Australia, you can contact WNA at www.womensnetwork. com.au. There are branches in most capital cities.

Supervision and Accountability

It is important to supervise the key areas of your business and put checklists in place to ensure accountability. Comprehensive accountability lists come as a part of the Bullet Proof Your Business program. Bullet Proof Your Business by Phoenix Global is a system of pre-written templates, documents and advice to make it easy for a business to protect itself.

If all parts of the system are put in place there is no reason anyone would be able to defraud that business.

Indeed, an investor is a business person even though she may not have a "shop front". You must treat your investments and even your domestic budget as a business in order to make the most of its cash flow.

Ironically, many people who contact Phoenix Global after experiencing a fraud such as intellectual property theft, embezzlement or product stolen, already knew about the Bullet Proof program but had not purchased it because they either hadn't got around to it or they didn't think fraud would happen to them.

They didn't think it would happen to them.

Why is Insurance Necessary?

If given the choice many people would not buy insurance. It's human nature to believe an accident won't happen because most of them happen to other people. Right? If we are preoccupied with what might go wrong, we might never take the risk of driving.

However, while we hope we will never need to use our insurance, we can drive with peace of mind knowing it is there. If something happens, at least that part of the unpleasantness is covered.

Business owners can protect themselves against fraud, but often are too busy to give it attention or it is simple matter of cash flow, which is another way of saying it is not a priority.

An investigation company can do a background check on a potential lover, business partner, employee or contractor. The greater the level of trust that is required, the more important and thorough the checking needs to be.

I recommend the use of a professional investigator to do a background check on anyone who is going to play a significant role in your business.

This includes lovers, because a lover's partnership becomes a business partnership. You have to consider who will pay for what in your private life until such time as the relationship becomes a union where all is "ours".

In the business arena there are areas of commerce and areas of investment. The same level of due-diligence is required of both.

In some circles, a prospectus is referred to as "a glorified advertisement".

While that may be harsh, it's true that a prospectus alone should not convince you to hand over money. You need to know the history of the people running the company, not just the bit in the blurb.

Due-diligence on a person may not reveal them to be a crook, but it could reveal potential areas of weakness or opportunities for conflict.

For example, John and Karen had the opportunity to put down an option payment on a piece of land preserving the price for 12 months. During that time, the value of the land skyrocketed due to a property boom.

John and Karen wanted to proceed with the purchase but did not qualify for a loan. They sought advice from their friends Mark and Louise because Mark and Louise had purchased several properties over the years they had known them.

Mark and Louise immediately recognized that the property should be purchased as there would be an immediate gain for their struggling friends. They offered to finance the deal in exchange for 50% of the profit when the block was resold.

Everyone was happy.

Due to Louise's experience in property transactions, she supervised the deal.

Karen began to feel that she was not being consulted about important decisions. Louise on the other hand did not consider the decisions important enough to require consultation.

The friendship was preserved by discussing each person's perspective, but the profitable venture could have resulted in a nasty dispute.

Lending money to friends will change the nature of the friendship.

Even when you have the means to assist someone financially, it is important to have an idea of how they perceive the deal. It is also important to be familiar with their history of handling finance.

Often as women we want to rescue someone. If it's in our power to fix their situation, we will often give before thinking about whether that is the right approach for them.

Sometimes it is not money they need but lessons on how to shop sensibly. Teaching someone life skills takes more effort than giving them $100 and your advice might be resented.

"The borrower is servant to the lender"

Proverbs 22:7.

If you want to lend someone money, just give it to them. If they pay it back it's a bonus and a credit to them, but it is more a credit to you to give and you will be less likely to ruin the friendship.

Most business misunderstandings do not have a good guy and a bad guy.

In most situations, people do not see themselves as the bad guy, so why would your adversary?

A real crook is subtle. He sets you up from the start with false documentation and history.

A private investigator can be necessary to find out a history that the fraudster would otherwise conceal. If he has not been caught previously there won't be a record, but private investigators can find things out that are off the record.

I loaned money to a currency trader we'll call "Butler". He came highly recommended. I went to his house and met his lovely wife and two young children. I checked that he was the owner of his house. He did not have a criminal record.

131

I conducted as much due-diligence as I knew how to do and could find no official, negative reports.

> Had he been a single man living in a flat, I would not have listened to him.

Even the Australian Securities and Investments Commission website indicated his company was registered and various papers had been filed, such as change of address etc. as necessary.

This benign list on the ASIC website made me think that I was dealing with a legitimate business.

Butler's associate even created a managed (mutual) fund, registered with ASIC with the appropriate prospectus documentation, just so that Butler could trade for it.

I did not think it unreasonable to assume that the authorities would not approve a fund without verifying how the income would be generated to produce returns for investors.

I was mistaken. The ASIC is not responsible for due-diligence. It approves prospectuses that have been correctly filled out. Investigation only occurs after complaints are made.

The farce was not the fault of the ASIC, although calling itself a "corporate regulator" I would have expected the regulating to start with due-diligence, but what do I know?

It is likely that the regulatory body in all first world countries can only offer limited evidence of due-diligence. As legislation changes from time to time, it is best to check what your state and Federal governments' policies are on investment protection.

The ASIC refers anyone who has breached the law to the Department of Public Prosecutions. The DPP in turn, has a policy of deterrence. This means they try to make an example of anyone who has wittingly or unwittingly breached the law.

The injustice here is that fraudsters are cunning and incriminate the unsuspecting business associate making sure they do not bring a complaint.

Brian rang me in great distress over losing $500,000 to a property fraud. It was one thing to lose the money but he was frightened that he would be implicated as well. He had signed papers as well as a check that had since disappeared. The fellow had been prosecuted, but he was not sure if he would be next.

Since ignorance is no defense, there is also little recourse for the victim who has unwittingly helped the fraudster. The most common is the "Ponzi" scheme by which an investor becomes a promoter because the returns are so good.

He doesn't realize that the trader is actually using the new money to pay returns to earlier investors.

Here is where the politically correct brigade would argue. We are not supposed to judge a person before they have done something and we are not supposed to consider a person a baddie because they happen to know one.

I'd rather err on the side of "if you lie down with dogs, you come up with fleas".

Romance is no different. If a young girl finds it exciting to hang around with a rebel, she is putting herself at risk. It's not about avoiding "the wrong side of the tracks" it's about not getting run over by the train!

If a prospective business or romantic partner is telling you about his success, you should see evidence of it. If they have a luxurious house, do a search to find out if they really own it.

Fraudsters are as manipulative as child molesters, frightening victims into silence by saying they have participated and are liable.

Searches

Searching court documents is a good way to find out if they are in dispute with anyone. Disputes will have an impact on their ability to deliver their side of the deal.

Some searches are consent driven. If you are going to do a business deal you can ask for their consent for certain searches. These include credit checks and police checks.

For a comprehensive background check it is best to use a professional investigator such as Phoenix Global. This company operates globally, which means it is more likely to uncover details that may not be known locally. If your prospect is offended at the idea, you should be cautious.

> Do not apologize for invading their privacy when they are asking you to trust them with your money.

In a similar way, guard your heart and be wary if your potential lover becomes indignant when asked about their past. This could be their secretive way of shaming you into not asking again.

I have no such shame.

In fact, I have found when the roles are reversed I sometimes share my setback because I know that it's better for them to hear it from me than from someone else. The result is usually admiration for my candor, and a confession of that person's own failed projects in the past.

> I'd rather do business with someone who has been burned than someone who has never made a mistake.

Now that I have been burned, I have created a set of standard questions that I ask in casual conversation. Without being rude, I simply tell the prospect that I have learned to be cautious and would they mind answering a few questions that are standard to my business. The genuine ones are usually obliging.

You can tactfully chat about personal things, listening for clues, e.g. how they feel about their personal relationships. I'm naturally someone who gets personal quickly and I have formed many great friendships this way.

I am aware that the politically correct view is that a person's personal life is private and is unrelated to their ability to provide service. I disagree. Do not fear that your nosiness will offend them and squash the deal. The break-up of a relationship has the potential to cause massive destruction to a business deal, especially if the spouse demands half of their business interests. Structuring is important in order to protect yourself.

Once again, it may not be politically correct to say so, but a person who is unfaithful to their life-partner is quite likely to be unfaithful to a business associate.

How they resist temptation is a character issue.

> If they can't keep their hands out of someone else's human candy jar, how will they keep their hands out of your account?

If your prospect finds someone more attractive to deal with, what's to stop them running off with the competition along with your I.P?

These problems might be personal but they have a way of crashing uninvited into your life!

Where possible, meet their family. Their spouse is a good starting point but if you are able to meet their extended family, it will reveal a lot about them.

I found the wife of a fellow was very hard to pin down. She avoided my efforts to have coffee with her, just to make friends. She claimed that by the time she cleaned the house it was time to pick up their daughter from pre-school. I know now, she did not want to let anything slip.

The following is a list of my standard questions (where possible try to incorporate them into normal conversation; no one likes being interrogated!):

- What is the worst thing that has happened to you in business?

- How did you handle it?

- Do you have any court or legal activity going on at the moment?

- Is anyone trying to undermine you? This can give away more than they expect because they may take the opportunity to pre-warn you about someone who might give you a negative report.

- Ask for their resume. Even if you are not giving them a job, it will provide you with a work history and skills you can verify.

- Do they operate any off-shore accounts? It may make them look clever, but it also gives them somewhere to hide your money one day.

- Who else are they currently in business with that could have an impact on your relationship or arrangement?

- What kind of asset protection do they currently have?

- Who will bear responsibility if the venture goes bad?

- Do you both agree on areas of vulnerability in the deal i.e. do you both understand the risks?

- How do they currently earn a living? This can produce vague answers. "This and that, here and there", are not acceptable responses.

- What are their hobbies? This is a nice way to find out if they have bad habits such as gambling.

- You need to know about their spouse's habits too. I once entered into an agreement with a couple not knowing the wife was not only an alcoholic but suffered with mental problems which caused her to sabotage the venture and the relationship.

Warning:

Don't become so desperate for the deal to go ahead that you lose your objectivity, making you vulnerable to being taken advantage of.

Another Risk is THE DREAM

Scammers feed our dreams, but we don't often realize our dreams are not realistic. They tell us what we want to hear. They flatter our "outside the square" thinking, praise us for not being content to run as "part of the pack", commend us for having the intelligence to do business with them.

 While it's good to not run with the pack, sometimes there is safety in numbers!

I'm not going to rain on anyone's parade, some people really do find "gold in them thar hills".

There are few short cuts. However, in day-to-day business, it's the mundane, faithful things that we do that make us better at what we do. I love the book "Acres of Diamonds" by Russell Herman Conwell.

We can go off on all sorts of tangents and not realize that with a little effort the rewards we seek are closer to home than we think.

Brian had quit his job as a professional in order to trade futures. He talked enthusiastically about how great futures trading was and how lots of money was there for the taking. His philosophy was: "When you make a little bit on a small amount you just do the same thing with a big amount."

He talked like an expert. However, in the same speech he invariably turned to how broke he was. In spite of not being successful at trading, it was his dream to make money from it. At the time, his industry was booming and there was a desperate shortage of top-tier professionals.

He could have been earning a salary well into the top tax bracket, saved a nest egg and then taken time off to trade with money that he could afford to risk. His degree of success would then show him whether to keep his job or keep trading. A perfect example of someone believing a dream that isn't working.

To know and not to do, is to not know!

Getting caught up with a charismatic, passionate person's delusions of grandeur will only cost you money and heartache. If you want to trade shares, future, options or currencies, fine. Do it with money you can afford to lose and build up your account.

Many people say to me, "Yes I know that, I know all about 95% of traders losing money... but that won't happen to me." What can I say? Maybe it won't...

Don't try to teach a pig to sing, you'll only get frustrated and it annoys the heck out of the pig.

In a radio interview, late November 2008, Robert Kiyosaki, made a comment along the lines of "study one thing and get good at it. Whether it be the stock market or property or anything else." He's right. You can't be too busy to study your particular investment instrument. Give it the respect it deserves if you expect to make money out of it.

If you don't want to trade yourself, research a fund that has a good track record, find out who the managers are and follow them if they leave. Beware of giving your money to another individual to invest. It is fraught with danger.

> **Never invest more than you can afford to lose!**

If you cannot afford to lose the money you are investing then you might be better off with a job. You can invest in upgrading your skills and look for a position that pays more.

Earn wages and find a conservative fund manager to watch your superannuation or 401k.

Beware of living the lifestyle of success before you've achieved it. By all means, look professional and buy quality when you can but remember; pride goes before a fall.

> **If your business cannot sustain your showing off, you are heading for trouble.**

On the other hand, beware of those who talk big but their car is held together with rubber bands.

Perhaps they take you to lunch and pull the old "I forgot my wallet" trick. Maybe they did, but start looking for other signs creating a "cluster" of warning signals.

When my husband and I were looking for our first investment property, we were being assisted by a salesman from a firm no longer in existence. He'd promised us lunch and a viewing of different properties. He "forgot" his wallet and so our lunch became a family meal deal at McDonalds!

Well, a simple phone call to a local real estate agent told me we could have bought a 4 bedroom house one street from the beach for the same price as the little unit overlooking a car park, which he was trying to sell.

Whether investing or considering a business venture, due-diligence is more than judging a person's handshake, reading a prospectus or doing a credit check.

Emotions

What emotions are you feeling when you anticipate an investment or business deal?

- Excited anticipation

- Anxiety

- Greed

- Exuberance

- Power

- Fear of loss

- Fear that it won't go through

- Fear that the person will not want to deal with me

- Attraction to the person

It's very important that you take time to examine the emotions you are feeling and try to work out where they come from.

Remember: Lust will send you bust.

Whether it is:

1. Lust for the person,

2. Lust for the deal, or

3. Lust for what you think the deal will bring you.

The Business Marriage

Business is like a marriage. To have success in both requires:

- Financial commitment

- Intimate knowledge of company intelligence

- Loyalty

- Confidentiality

- Understanding of one another's strengths and weaknesses.

- Knowledge of others they are in relationship with.

- Knowledge and understanding of the demands others place on each of you.

- Grace and forgiveness.

- Some people cannot commit to their personal life partner so how committed will they be to you?

- The break-up of each type of relationship comes at a cost. Discover as much as possible about someone before taking the plunge.

- You also need to know about yourself and how you react, your hot buttons that leave you open to manipulation.

- If it is not the first business venture or relationship, then it is likely you each have "issues" that will affect how you respond in the new venture.

 Get healed, get smart, get the deal and people checked out then get on with it!

141

Remember...

1. Lust can send you bust, even in business.

2. Don't assume someone else is keeping an eye on financial controls. There may be someone keeping an eye on the finances, but for the wrong reasons.

3. Keep control of the accounts. I've heard that as successful as Oprah is, just like Lynette, she still controls the cash flow of her business. If they can keep on top of it, we can too.

4. Beware of mistaking dumping for delegating. The creative side of your business may be what excites you but don't be fooled into neglecting the "boring bits".

Take the Princess Warrior Challenge

- ⚔ Have I bullet proofed my business?

- ⚔ Are my assets protected?

- ⚔ Have I done everything I can to investigate the person, the deal and been honest with myself?

- ⚔ What is the number of Phoenix Global, Corporate and Private Investigators, who can investigate all over the world if necessary? 1300 475 515

- ⚔ Calling from outside Australia 61 7 5580 5554

- ⚔ Who do I quote as my referrer to get privileged rates? Trish Jenkins!!!

PART 3:

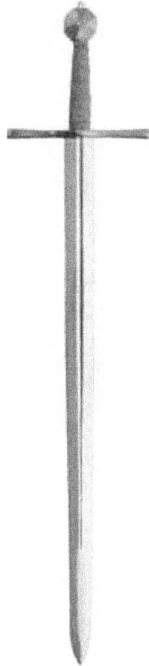

MOVING   FORWARD

Chapter Eleven
Self Assessment...

Business and Life...
Examine Your Heart

"The heart is deceitfully wicked above all things, who can know it?"

Jeremiah 17:9

Ooh, that doesn't sound very nice, does it? What about the spiritual, touchy feely, "I am wonderful" clichés?

Well, you are wonderful. You are spiritual. Touchy, feely stuff is lovely. However:

 Self-delusion is what makes us vulnerable to the "nasties" who would manipulate our desire to feel good about ourselves.

Truth hurts, but knowing the truth is what sets us free.

As I have said, every person who comes into our lives leaves footprints on our heart.

In some coastal towns, early in the morning, a grader goes along the beach and smoothes out the sand, removing sharp objects and rubbish. Where it had been misshapen and made uneven by the feet of the previous day, it is made pristine as on the first morning of creation.

If only we could smooth over our hearts like that so every new experience is untainted by previous hurts.

How is it that intelligent people can get carried away by love, lust or greed? Our experiences and our natural inclinations taint the way we interpret what is presented to us. Our heart makes us see things the way we want to see them instead of the way they really are.

> Our heart is the filter of the things we let closest to us.

O Treacherous Heart!

We all have a friend who has fallen in love with someone we knew was "bad news". We watched them go from an exciting flirtation where they wouldn't stop telling us about how wonderful he was, to an obsession where we were ignored altogether.

Helplessly we watched as their lives began to revolve around the new love in their life. All other interests, the things they had previously enjoyed and achieved, were abandoned. Then we pick up the pieces of our heart-broken friend after what we predicted would happen, happened.

> Few people consciously decide to get caught up in a scam. It happens by seduction and deception.

We can usually see the warning signs for others, but ironically we when it comes to our own warning signs, they take on a cloak of invisibility.

Our heart is responsible. Whether love, lust or greed, it is always the heart that lets us down; not the head.

Make a decision that you are an overcomer and not a victim. This attitude is your "Seat of Personal Power".

When we want something to be true badly enough, all sound judgment goes straight out the window.

It is very important to know and carry out I call the 11th Commandment:

Thou Shalt Not Kid Thyself!

It's not an easy thing to honestly examine our heart. If we filter the influences over our heart then we will be better protected and our heart will serve us well. Good will always come out of what you have been through.

The next step is to devise a plan to maintain a winning attitude.

You may not be able to do that until you've followed some of the following strategies:

It starts with examining your heart on a regular basis. Sit quietly and wait with a pencil and paper. Think about the various aspects of your life and try to objectively assess the emotions that arise.

What is coming up?

Sadness, Bitterness, Unforgiveness, Anger, Frustration, Desire, Lust, Despair, Disappointment, Uneasiness, Shame...

What about positive emotions like:

Love, Satisfaction, Contentment, Excitement, Peace, Joy?

It will help to have a journal so that you can express what you feel about each situation as you think of it.

Take one situation at a time. Try to identify when it started. How did you meet? What did you try to find out about the person? Now you may be feeling angry that you didn't find out more. It's time to acknowledge that. Forgiving yourself for being human will help you smile about it in the future.

🛡️ **Revenge may be a dish best served cold but it will still give you indigestion!**

Listen for any memories of warning signals, a feeling of unease? A friend's caution?

Take each stage of the experience and first acknowledge and own the part where you failed yourself, repent to yourself and release yourself from the guilt of self-reproach.

Sometimes when we are angry, we can turn that anger on ourselves. "If only I had this or that, it wouldn't have happened!"

According to Os Hillman in his excellent daily devotional TGIF (Today God Is First):

"Whenever we have expectations of another person and those expectations do not materialize, our tendency is to get angry. The source of the anger is often the fear that the unmet expectation will negatively impact us. We fear that our finances, our well-being, our image, or any number of things may be impacted by the unmet expectation." Marketplace Leaders "Checking Under the Hood" November 24th 2007.

It is important to find out the source of our fear. It's like peeling an onion; one thought leads back to another until the center of the fear is identified. When you drill down, it can then be reframed.

🛡️ **What doesn't kill you makes you stronger!**

Now dig deep and look for anything good that may have come out of the negative experience. One of my favorite teachers of life is Joyce Meyer; all her books are helpful.

Her childhood was marred by shocking sexual abuse that affected her ability to function normally as an adult. She was mistrustful and had control issues.

Today she ministers to women all over the world who have suffered the same pain. Her healing came through discovering the unconditional love of God.

She took her experiences and laid them at the feet of Jesus. It took time, but now she is even grateful for the experience she had because she is able to help so many other women become free.

 What is there about your experience that has produced, or could produce, something good?

Write it down.

When you reframe your experience you give it a new meaning for your life.

For example, losing your job provides you with an opportunity to start a new adventure.

The end of a love affair means you can do the things he was not interested in.

The loss of money will hopefully help you resolve to get the next venture checked out professionally.

Cognitive Dissonance... What the?

Cognitive dissonance occurs when the mind is expected to hold two conflicting thoughts at the same time. It's just not possible and stress is generated requiring imaginative justification for the inconsistency.

For example, a successful person may hold the opinion that they are a good investor. They may be so good that it is not possible for them to be defrauded. They are too clever for that.

When they eventually are defrauded, they often will not accept that their money has disappeared. This explains the desperate cling many people have to a scam such as the common Nigerian scheme.

It is unacceptable for the money to be gone and so they become delusional. Even if there was no fraud and they lost money, it cannot be inconsistent with their opinion of themselves and so they find a way to face the unacceptable. The conclusion: "It must be someone else's fault!"

Until you face reality and accept responsibility for your error of judgment, regardless of whose "fault" it was, you will not move forward.

The next chapter will help you detox your mind in order to "sharpen your sword."

Chapter Twelve

Bouncing Back...

Cutting the Crap with Your Sword!

Hawaii, 2003 at the annual Bob Harrison Increase Event.

It was morning tea time and I was browsing one of the book tables. (Correction, Americans do not have morning tea, they have coffee with cream or half-milk, half-cream and they have iced tea, something I'll never get used to).

As I scanned the table, my eye fell on a book title that I immediately snatched up.

"If 'How-To's Were Enough, We'd All Be Skinny, Rich and Happy!" by Brian Klemmer. I didn't even turn the book over before exclaiming, "I have to have this!"

The slim, bearded gentleman manning the table said softly, "You can have that". Puzzled and grateful I thanked him and we chatted briefly. He was the author.

Later I was to see him walk on the stage as a key-note speaker for the conference. I was to learn that he has a massive world-wide business, training achievers in how to think differently to solve problems and change their circumstances.

I did not know at that stage how much I would need to use that kind of thinking in my not so distant future.

Note: International readers, "crap" means excuses, rubbish or poop - apply where appropriate.

This chapter offers some strategies to help you prepare for change. It is NOT meant to replace professional therapy or medication. Deep pain thrusts us into a journey that can enrich us or ruin us. I wanted an 'express' lane through the pain so that I could be "successful" again.

However, while I found strategies that broke the back of the pain, I didn't find shortcuts.

Humans are deep and complex, so true change can only come gradually with constant adjustments; much like the turning of an ocean liner as opposed to the quick spinning of a little boat.

> Know yourself and you will see others differently. Be kind to yourself.

It is important to learn how you function, what makes you tick and what hot buttons trigger your pain. If you don't know yourself, you cannot strengthen or protect your weak spots.

A broken arm requires attention and protection followed by gradual restoration of strength. Should emotions and finances be any different?

A clever quote or deep revelation may motivate you to a decision, but a lasting change is the result of making that decision daily and consciously changing habits until they become a natural part of your perspective.

Give yourself time, but persist.

The Decision

In April, 2010, I wrestled with this manuscript. Part of me was terrified to face it. I kept putting off its completion. I was frustrated, scared and unhappy.

I didn't want to go public with my imprisonment, but I knew I could not release and promote a book without it being part of my story. I was also angry because in my heart I already knew the decision I had to make, and therefore resented not really having a choice.

Can we choose something we don't really have a choice about? Yes.

I eventually decided that even if I did have a choice, I would still choose to go ahead with it. This was a healing and strengthening decision in my journey.

> *"Life and Death are set before you, blessing and cursing: therefore choose life so that you and your children may live!"*
>
> Deuteronomy 3 0:19b (paraphrased)

Had I chosen to retreat, it would have meant death: Death to my confidence and death to my dreams. The curse of giving up may well have been followed by the death of my marriage and the blighting of my children.

Why? Because poison spreads, it begins in one area of life, and then infects another, then another.

I wasn't having that!

Do areas of your life feel cursed? Choose life. Make the better yet difficult, day-by-day decisions that are for your good.

Self-pity is a con artist. It is the easier, tempting choice but it brings destruction.

It may be that your depth of despair means you do not care; but your life is not just about you, is it?

Once The Decision was made, my freedom and joy returned, along with a motivating sense of purpose. It was a powerful moment. I treasure that moment. I draw on that moment regularly because experience has shown me that even though I can get filled with a sense of passion and conviction, it also leaks away...

Leakage

I regularly leak. I leak motivation, I leak patience, I leak love and I leak confidence.

I leak because I am human.

I leak because I am damaged.

I leak because I care too much what people think and I fear their disapproval.

I am aware of these weaknesses; these illusory perceptions.

Yet it is in my weakness, I am made strong.

Again, I make The Decision and that regains my perspective, and fear melts away.

This is the point where faith in The Universe and faith in God differ. The Law of Attraction says, "Weakness attracts weakness", but the God of the universe says,

"Your weakness is a platform for My strength."

Vision and Purpose

My perspective comes from my vision. A worthwhile vision has a purpose. My purpose is to empower women to make wiser financial and romantic choices. An empowered woman, with a purpose, is able to make choices that change the destiny of her family and impact the wider community.

You've heard the saying, "Give a man a fish and you'll feed him for a day; teach a man to fish and you'll feed him for a lifetime?" Well a wise woman added, "Teach a woman to fish and she'll feed the whole village."

Consider the following:

Candy Lightner founded MADD (Mothers Against Drunk Driving) after a repeat drunk driver killed her daughter. Today MADD is a movement impacting a nation!

Hetty Johnston founded "Bravehearts" which tackles the issue of child sex abuse in the community.

Debbie Kilroy founded "Sisters Inside" which supports and helps rehabilitate women who are or have been in prison, and their families. Debbie is the subject of the book "Kilroy was here" by Kris Olsson (Bantam, Sydney 2005.)

I'll have more to say about how prison damages women and how society actually fosters repeat offenses in my next book. I thank God for women like Debbie. "That which you do to the least of these, you are doing to Me" – Jesus.

There are so many more. I'd love to hear your stories of women who have overcome adversity, recovered and gone on to impact the wider community as a result!

You may feel that your pain is too great to even think about anyone else. Let me reassure you that there is a season to grieve, but at some point you must choose Life so you can make your way out of the sludge.

Learn about yourself and then look outward.

Whatever I think I might lose by putting myself "out there" - pride, personal dignity, favor, opportunities; it is all shallow and selfish compared to the potential impact of my undignified words.

Your life has a purpose. Live with purpose, on purpose. You matter. You are needed. There is a role for you. If you have trouble finding your purpose, look outside yourself and help someone else with something, anything to start with. What can you do to enhance someone else's life? Don't be choosy, just try something however small, keep at it and your purpose will find you.

Strangely, the fear now serves me. When I speak publicly, I cannot afford to be superficial. It is easily identified. My very "weakness" provides the strength of my message. I'd rather be vulnerable and open in order to deliver something of real worth to another's life.

 You matter. We need you.

Taking Action

In addition to "The Decision," I am sharing some strategies that continue to help me, as well as my "30 Day Challenge for Change". The strategies are not exhaustive and you don't need to be Wonder Woman to do them. You just need to take your time and be honest with yourself about you and your relationships.

 Right thinking is vital.

Let me caution you against assuming you are already thinking right, simply because you are thinking the same way as the people in your organization, MLM business or corporation.

Those who hold positions you aspire to are still human and may not always practice what they are teaching their protégés to do and think. This knowledge should not make you bitter; it should remind you to continue to think for yourself.

> Mentors are vital, but human. Don't put them on a pedestal as they will probably disappoint you at some stage.

Continue to read widely but again, retain the practice of thinking for yourself. Otherwise you risk being manipulated by a "life coach" or, for the spiritual, sliding into a cult. Contrary to popular cultural opinion, the Christian believer is actually obliged to examine and test what is taught. God loves a seeker of truth.

You may be thinking at this point, that God isn't real. Just because you think it, doesn't make it true. Perhaps what you've been taught about Him was faulty? Just a thought.

> Blind faith in what a person says leads to deception and disables you in your own walk.

You don't have to agree with your mentor or protégé on all points. Nor do you have to agree with all the points you are reading here. This book is the result of what has worked for me. If even a small portion of it helps you on your journey, then it is worth it.

Conflicts of Interest

> When it comes to money, somebody else's opinion must remain their opinion.

The fact is, nobody will take responsibility for the consequences if you do follow their advice, suggestion or manipulative demands.

When you are successful, you will always meet people who feel entitled to remonstrate with you; be it a parent, boss, mentor or leader.

If you decide to engage in business with a mentor, go in with your eyes open. Do not see them through rose-colored glasses simply because they have helped you in other arenas of life. Communicate and clarify the relationship in its new context.

Single mother, Pamela, had developed her own business but felt she needed help to expand. She subsequently went into partnership with a previous employer. When her partner persisted in treating her like a subordinate, withdrawing cash from the business without notice, Pamela called a meeting to address the issue. While not technically fraud, her partner was still taking advantage.

"From that time on nothing I did was right in her eyes, and eventually I realized that the relationship was to my detriment." said Pamela.

The partnership dissolved in an expensive mess.

It took Pamela two years to get past the hurt and betrayal she felt. The same amount of time, psychologists say, it takes to recover from a death or major trauma.

My advice to Pamela was to not just see things from the other person's point of view, but understand that person is just as vulnerable and flawed as the rest of us. Pamela had projected qualities onto her partner that were unrealistic.

What we perceive as bad leadership can actually be good for us.

Some bosses, or clients if you are the boss, can be very demanding and unreasonable, yet doesn't this quality make us stretch to do better?

Don't waste time feeling hurt and betrayed. OK, you might need some time to grieve, but look for the lesson as soon as you can. When you find it, your negative perception will change to a positive. This will take practice but eventually it will happen on its own. How we interpret an event, is what helps or hurts us, not the event in itself.

I have several mentors in various arenas of life, but I am under no illusions about them.

My favorite mentors are those who have humility and who do not care who gets the "glory".

I don't have to agree with them to be able to respect them even in their imperfections. Yet I am not so arrogant as to dismiss the good advice they do give. Furthermore, while I prefer those who are aware of their weaknesses, I can still learn from those who are not.

Here are 9 steps to assist you in getting over setbacks and betrayals:

1. Face the fear

"No passion so effectually robs the mind of all its powers of acting and reasoning as fear."   Edmund Burke

Look your worst case scenario full in the face.

Imagine that scenario is a horrible garden that you must walk through, but know there will be an exit.

Ask yourself, what is the worst that can happen?

Loss of reputation?

Loss of money?

Humiliation?

Loss of your home?

Loss of your friends?

Death?

Imprisonment?

Be honest. Do you need to get a referral to a professional counselor? Can you access some simple NLP techniques to reframe how you are viewing the situation?

For those who are spiritual, this is a time to get a "word" from God. Personalize it like I did with Psalm 91. It was mine. Stand on it and stay close to Him.

Things come to pass and they pass.

2. Take responsibility

I've met leaders who talk about their trusting everybody as though it's a virtue. A kind of "to the pure all things are pure" attitude.

The problem is that being too trusting is actually the trait of a fool. A person in a position of responsibility such as a company director or a pastor has an obligation to verify what he or she is told.

You have a responsibility to those you manage and care for to never be too busy to verify the facts.

You don't need to beat yourself up but it is important that you acknowledge any role you played in your own setback. Stop focusing on the person who did you wrong and look at how you might have enabled them to wrong you. It might be greed, hastiness, naiveté or lust.

Understand the ways your background may have caused a vulnerability to a particular kind of manipulation. Think about your situation. What old beliefs now need to change?

In my situation, I had to readjust my understanding of loyalty. Loyalty is often touted as a great virtue, but it is also a virtue that makes a fraudster so very successful.

Loyalty just happens to be one of my flaws as it takes an awful lot for me to stop believing in someone. In fact, it took a liquidator sitting me down and literally proving that I had been lied to, before I could stop.

I have learned my lesson. I now realize people are fallible and do not waste emotional energy depending on their integrity.

However, I caution you to be careful not to write off a whole group of people based on one person's actions. That is simply prejudice.

> Not all Nigerians are corrupt even though Nigeria is the source of many internet scams.

3. Repentance

It might sound religious, but there is a reason why repentance is so powerful. Acknowledging your failure sets you free from the torment it brings.

Repentance has several meanings

- To change one's mind – change the way you previously thought about something.

- To turn away from an action or attitude.

Rather than claim victim status, you will be empowered by acknowledging where you went wrong and can begin taking steps to ensure it is less likely to happen again.

Do you need to accept that greed made you a willing participant?

Were you deceived by your desires? Has your turmoil caused you to treat someone unkindly?

> Take responsibility, but only for your part. Do not take responsibility for someone else's decision.

Know where your part finishes and theirs begins.

This was crucial in my healing from financial disaster. People did what I did because I had been successful. They lost money because my investment lost money. I felt dreadful that they made a decision based on my influence. However, it was their decision.

I had to make the distinction for my own sanity. It actually broke condemnation off my life.

Condemnation is when you do not feel "free". Even after repenting of it, you still feel guilty.

4. Forgiveness

Forgive yourself; forgive the fraud. Forgive the people who let you down or judged you. They could be family or friends.

The hardest people for me to forgive were in two groups:

- The friends who turned out to be fair-weather friends.

- People in positions of leadership who turned to water. It's easy to give advice when it's not your issue, but when it visits you, be assured your reaction is being observed by those you influence.

- Cowardice is more noticeable in a leader.

My ability to forgive came after I imagined myself in their shoes. As I get older and make mistakes, I can only have compassion for those who blow it. These days I am grateful for the changes that have occurred.

Young ones can be very judgmental, they have the luxury of not having had enough time to stuff things up as much as their elders!

Would I do it all again? Not in a pink fit!!!

Forgiveness is easier said than done.

5. Surrender

Forgiveness requires surrender. Let it go. Abandon your need for justice and let the One who judges justly take over. There are some good NLP mental exercises that can help you release yourself. The surrender of judgment and hate releases blessings and peace into your mind and life.

The most effective technique is not a technique.

It's not easy... But it gets easier with practice.

It's not popular... Sometimes I'd rather vomit than do it.

It works in prison, in business, in family, in life... Every time.

The more I do it... The faster I get free.

It's not NLP... It's

 Pray for your enemies!

It sounds crazy until you try it. Jesus said to do it (among other radical things. Matt 5:44). If you give it a try, you will find that the pain of what they have done to you recedes.

When I do this I pray for God to give me His perspective of the one who wronged me. I pray for their health, finances, family, mind, soul and anything else I can think of.

By the time I'm done I'm no longer a victim. I am free, I am empowered. I am even moved by compassion and pity for them, even if they are really "bad".

 That is what forgiveness feels like.

6. Trust

Trust in yourself, even though you may have failed. Often our first instinct was right, but we second guess because we want something more.

Don't beat yourself up for learning the hard way; just learn. Trust your future is turning out all right. Trust in your inner Warrior, Princess!

"Beware the Leader who has no limp."

7. Shore up

Strengthen yourself with good things, such as positive CD messages and quality friends and associates. Surround yourself with genuine people and dwell on the positive things in your life and a "force field" impervious to deception begins to build.

Don't listen to sad songs or watch pessimistic movies. Stick to uplifting material. Guard what you see and what you hear.

Remove negativity, even asking your friends not to talk about certain subjects. Avoid those who lament "What am I going to do?" or specifically ask them to stop saying it around you.

There is no answer at that point and it will drain you.

If necessary, filter your friends.

8. Give

I've heard wealth creation "gurus" say, "Make your money first and then make a difference". I disagree. Create the habit of giving now. If you don't give now, you won't give then. You will make the excuse that you still don't have enough.

Guess what? There will never be enough before you start!

Giving will build something worth more than money into your life. Then, when you are wealthy, you will have the experience to give in a more effective way.

Just start to give. Your Money. Your Time. Your Talent. It's good for you on so many levels.

9. Look forward

Take some time to consider your goals and of course, your vision.

If you are a goal setter as many successful businesswomen are, your goals are a good starting point. Take some time out to re-examine them and the motives behind them.

I encourage you to think higher than serving you and yours. Have a vision that will leave this world a better place.

Maslow Modified

Acclaimed Psychologist, Abraham Maslow is known for his Hierarchy of Human Needs. Our most basic needs are biological; the highest need is "self-actualization."

The individual is unable to progress to higher stages until the need of the previous stage is met.

- Self-actualization - personal growth and fulfillment
- Aesthetic
- Cognitive
- Belongingness
- Safety
- Biological

The list is realistic and in a logical, humanistic order. It is also all about "Self". If we truly want to grow and lose that nagging dissatisfaction, we must begin to focus more outwardly. I didn't say neglect our responsibilities or be a doormat.

Pop psychology would have us find the answer in ourselves but that is only partly true.

Be self-aware but not selfish. We have to look out for others and care for our environment. We are born with a sense of purpose and that purpose is not about self-gratification.

What if Maslow added "enabling others" to the top of the pyramid?

I'd rather see it running up the side touching every level, but that sounds just like a woman, doesn't it?

Every one of Maslow's stages requires other people helping us meet our need. From cradle to grave we are interdependent with each other and our environment.

I've created a new theory of needs to compare with Maslow.

Imagine the following:

Self-focused Inward vision		Whole Vision Self within community
	Self-actualization ⟷ See God in others	
	Aesthetic ⟷ Humility	
	Cognitive ⟷ Respect	
	Belongingness ⟷ Adoption	
	Safety ⟷ Champion others	
	Biological ⟷ Sharing Basic Needs	

Let's do it well!

30 Day Challenge for Change

- Prepare... Cleanse your mind. Identify things to cut out and things to do.
- Write a list of everything in your life that you can be thankful for.
- Take the main points and try to fit them onto the back of a business card. Prepare 3 such cards.

1. Place one card beside your bed.
2. Keep one on your person, either in your pocket or purse.
3. Place the third at your work station.

Ask two or three close friends to call you every few days to encourage you and keep you on track. Accountability is a great motivator. Those with a faith should engage an intercessory prayer service. I am covered daily by www. businessblessings.com.

Detox

Identify things in your life that are not good for your mental state. Choose not to watch TV. Can you go without it? You are probably a busy person so it shouldn't be hard to turn it off. Don't listen to the radio unless it is positive music.

When you speak, listen to your conversation.

If necessary take a little MP3 recorder with you to listen to your default conversation. How many times do you complain or say something negative?

I'm not saying we should suffer injustice, just quit harping for 30 days. Don't talk on about somebody owing you money or doing you wrong. You will frown less which will make you look younger, healthier and be less of a bore to your friends!

If you cannot decide if something is good for you, ask yourself:

- Does it make me feel like a better person?

- Does it make me want to be a better person?

- Does it leave me feeling dirty?

- Does it contain positive role models e.g. a TV show?

- Does this person bring out the gossip in me?

- Do I feel stupid or inadequate around this person?

- Do I want to be more like what I am looking at or listening to?

It will actually do your soul good to fast from things that feed negativity.

Don't indulge in the things that make you feel sluggish.

Build

- Set your alarm 10 minutes earlier.

- Wake up and reach for your "Thankful card". Think about those things as you lie there.

- There are 3 1 chapters in the ancient wisdom book of Proverbs, one for each day of the month. Read it over breakfast.

- If one point stands out, keep mindful of it throughout the day.

- Take an inspiring book to work with you and read it in your lunchtime instead of chatting with your colleagues, or chat with them after you've read a few pages on your own.

- If your friends start to talk negatively, tactfully change the subject. This will not always work as some people were born, then baptized in lemon juice. (Some people have an expression of permanent disapproval. They are the kind of people whose nose is screwed up and whose mouth resembles the rear end of a cat.)

- Make sure you eat a lot of fruit and vegetables.

- Enjoy just a 20 minute walk or jog each day. Call it "my thinking time". Get outside and look at nature. Sunshine gets a lot of bad press but it is a source of vitamin D and makes you feel good. Mark Kenway of www.lifeafterliquidation. com recommends "Sunshine therapy" to help get your peace and joy back. Be sure to use sunscreen and hat, get out, soak up the sun and look at nature. Avoid the hottest part of the day, carry a bottle of water and enjoy the rejuvenation it brings.

- Each day say or do something nice and unexpected for someone you do not know very well.

- After two weeks, resume watching TV. As you do, look for the message behind the message.

- Look at the values being promoted in the TV shows you do watch. What are the qualities the program is telling you are important? Looks, sex appeal? What role do females play? Are they decorative? Intelligent? Plain? Fat? Promiscuous?

Live in Reality

What else are you exposed to that is not the truth?

When I visited Los Angeles I saw more Latin American people than I had expected. The TV shows I had watched did not accurately represent the true landscape of the city. I was particularly impressed with a McDonald's worker who I could not understand, but who persisted until she had served me successfully. Courageous. Talk about stepping out of a comfort zone!

What are your children watching on television? What wrong impressions are they receiving? Have you watched MTV with them, listened to the words? Have you really looked at what girls wear in video clips? Is your child being influenced by the sexual lies of pop culture? This is what you must wear to be popular; this is what you must do to be "cool" What destructive deception!

When my eldest daughter wants to download a song we go to the internet and look up the lyrics. Sometimes she'll exclaim "Oh mom, that's rude!" That is a teachable moment where I take the opportunity to discuss why talented idiots would write such crap (choose your definition). Is it passion, dysfunctional issues or once again, to get noticed so it will SELL? I tend towards thinking it's the latter.

My daughters once asked me about Halloween, "Why are kids dressing up and asking strangers for treats?" It was hard to explain why children were allowed to do something they are normally warned against i.e. taking sweets from strangers.

However, the businesswoman in me surfaced and I went with it, explaining that Australia's interest in Halloween had been minimal until the media and business realized it was another sales opportunity! Halloween was once a tradition about scaring bad spirits away. Now it's a massive marketing campaign with the bonus of giving children cavities... but wait ...you also get...Nightmares!

Thanks.

It is not easy to filter what we are exposed to. The media is an integral part of our lives. It is a great servant but a reckless, callous dictator. Pro-actively analyzing and filtering what we are exposed to will sharpen our discernment and ability to think independently.

You will begin to notice a difference in your outlook, become more productive and inevitably less stressed.

Chapter Thirteen

Turning Setbacks...

...Into Success

"We are familiar with someone calling themselves a self-made millionaire but no-one ever refers to themselves as a self-made failure!"

Ps. Mark Ramsey

The University of Adversity cannot be avoided by anyone fulfilling their purpose.

A great book that helped me overcome adversity is John Maxwell's "Failing Forward". Maxwell makes the point that schools teach us that failing is bad. However, true failure is not learning the lesson. Some people berate themselves, while others always blame someone or something else. True failure is not learning the lesson.

 Failure is often just a matter of perception.

Prevention is not guaranteed even for the almost perfect.

Failure can be the result of mismanagement or misfortune or both. Good management can protect us against some misfortunes.

International speaker and pastor, Mark Ramsey often says,

"Manage your money, or manage a money crisis. Manage your marriage, or manage a marriage crisis."

You must see your setbacks as lessons and focus on the good that can come of it.

INGREDIENTS FOR FAILURE

- Failure to manage your temper can result in bigger failure.

- Refusing to entertain another point of view.

- Taking legal action is the result of failing to negotiate or failing to protect yourself adequately.

- Self-righteousness.

- Poverty is not always about material needs. Poverty of grace is a desert.

- Complacency.

- Lack of accountability. Have a couple of people in your life you trust to help you stay on track.

- Not separating yourself from the action that didn't work.

It's easy for the rest of us to judge someone when we believe their sins exceed our own. However, the only difference between them and us could be time and opportunity.

Ironically, I sometimes feel anger when I think about people who have not been gracious to those who have failed.

I feel judgmental about their judgment!

It's an insidious trait because it carries with it a sense of indignation, superiority and self-righteousness that is difficult to correct and cannot be argued with.

"If you judge people, you have no time to love them."

- Mother Theresa

TIPS FOR DEALING WITH FAILURE

- ⟨ Keep a sense of humor. Don't take yourself too seriously.
- ⟨ Must be able to laugh at yourself.
- ⟨ Beware that anxiety in the heart can cause depression and affect your health.
- ⟨ Get freedom from shame of failure.
- ⟨ Look for the lesson.
- ⟨ Identify anything good from the experience.
- ⟨ Change what you believe your experience means for your life.
- ⟨ Know when to quit or change.
- ⟨ Hear from God, or your instincts, for when it's time to move on.

Misplaced loyalty can waste decades of your life.

Carol, 57, had a lifelong dream of teaching little children in a third world country. However, people who genuinely cared about her feared she wasn't "up to it". This made her question if her desire was "God's will".

I told her, "For goodness sake, go! Have an adventure, God won't mind and you might even do some good!"

She went and her life is richer for it!

The author of this little story is unknown to me, but I love it.

WHEN YOUR HUT'S ON FIRE...

The only survivor of a shipwreck was washed up on a small, uninhabited island. He prayed feverishly for God to rescue him. Every day he scanned the horizon for help, but none seemed forthcoming.

Exhausted, he eventually managed to build a little hut out of driftwood to protect himself from the elements, and to store his few possessions.

One day, after scavenging for food, he arrived home to find his little hut in flames, with smoke rolling up to the sky. He felt the worst had happened, and everything was lost.

He was stunned with disbelief, grief, and anger.

He cried out, "God! How could you do this to me?"

Early the next day, he was awakened by the sound of a ship approaching the island! It had come to rescue him!

"How did you know I was here?" asked the weary man of his rescuers.

"We saw your smoke signal," they replied.

The Moral of This Story: It's easy to get discouraged when things are going bad, but we shouldn't lose heart, because God is at work in our lives, even in the midst of our pain and suffering.

Remember, next time your little hut seems to be burning to the ground; it just may be a smoke signal that summons the Grace of God.

You never know who feels as if their hut is on fire today.

Chapter Fourteen Legacy:

What Are You Doing That Actually Matters?

"Whenever I watch TV and I see those poor starving kids all over the world, I can't help but cry. I mean I would love to be skinny like that, but not with all those flies and death and stuff."

[The above quote is attributed to a certain pop star that I am not brave enough to name.]

Natural Selection and Social Darwinism

According to All about Science website, "Social Darwinism" is an application of the theory of natural selection to social, political, and economic issues.

In its simplest form, Social Darwinism follows the mantra of 'the strong survive', including human issues. What has this to do with economics? Fraudsters are devotees of the theory of "Survival of the Fittest". They see their taking advantage as "the law of the jungle".

We may be appalled at that idea, however many in society hold the same view even though they may not break the law. "The problem with the starving Africans," pontificated Harold, (middle aged bank manager) at a business networking dinner, "is that when we feed them, they get healthy and breed and then there are more of them to feed! Helping them just makes the problem worse." (I half expected him to snort and add "eh, what?" like an English lord).

"Unless you are one of them," answered my husband.

There are those who believe the poor are that way because they are lazy or stupid; that giving charity only encourages sloth.

It is all very well to talk about "teaching a man to fish, rather than giving him one". That's fine as long as he doesn't starve before the lesson is over!

If you are truly concerned about misdirected charity, and are not just looking for an excuse to preserve your own prosperity, simply support charities that will gladly show you how the funds are used.

For example, the "She" Rescue Home not only rescues girls from sex slavery, it teaches them skills that will enable them to create a good living for themselves and others.

The Watoto Children's Choir travels the world singing and raising funds to support villages created to house and teach children orphaned by war and HIV AIDS. The children are being trained to not just survive, but to be the next generation of leaders for a peaceful Uganda.

There are clubs such as Zonta and Soroptimist International, which already have amazing programs in place to help women and girls all over the world. A club is a great way for you to make friends and increase your business network.

Maybe the reason we haven't found a cure for cancer or AIDS is because only a small percentage of the world's population is well fed and prosperous enough to study.

Who knows what potential lies wasted in the pool of the desperate and starving?

Social Darwinism provided an explanation for slavery (defrauding a person's freedom) and selfishness in the past. While it may be "human nature" to use force to subject a person or race to another's will, it doesn't make it right. By the way, slavery is one of the biggest industries in the world today. I saw a Cambodian slave trader interviewed in a documentary. When asked how he could bring himself to procure little girls for prostitution, he shrugged and said, "It's just business." Social Darwinism at work.

Today we use different language to protect our prosperity and justify our self-absorption. "It's their culture." "It's only wrong according to Western values." "My little bit won't make any difference."

The irony is that there will never be enough to satisfy the person who does not give. There is no greater feeling than to do something for someone who cannot do anything in return. Giving provides a satisfaction and even a joy that is hard to describe.

I promise you, the feeling you will get from making a difference in someone else's life, will give you more satisfaction than any expensive trinket.

 You won't need stress relief medication when your life is less about you and your own "fulfillment".

Go beyond even the idea that the Universe or God will reward you, for even in that lies a selfish motive. The true reward is in what it makes of you. Anything else you reap is a bonus. No fraud can take that away.

Our journey has never been without giving. Even before we started to make "real" money, we gave at least 10% of our income away. When we really started prospering, we were inspired by R.G. Le Tourneau, author of "Of Men and Mountains". We gave more than we lived on and didn't tell people about it.

When things turned upside down and we lost everything, the liquidator was astounded and genuinely puzzled about why we had given away so much. We may have been defrauded, but the lives we changed were worth the loss and suffering. Cars and houses are nice, but they don't last. Feeding those desires only creates greater hunger for them.

It's time to be a woman of wisdom. Life is short. If you want to make your life count for something, take a risk, but take a calculated risk. If I'd been more careful, I would still be growing my portfolio and giving even more. However, I've not been stopped.

A Final Story:

While on a business trip to Sydney in January 2002 I had occasion to attend the birthday party of a business associate I normally only communicated with by phone and email.

Although I didn't know many people, it was a friendly gathering of like-minded individuals.

All of us were involved in creating wealth in one form or another. I found myself seated next to an attractive couple in their late twenties.

Mark and Penelope were very chic, from their expensive shoes, perfect hair, designer outfits, to their perfect smiles. They had it down pat, in other words, the picture of young successful entrepreneurs.

Having been a photographer, I appreciate beauty. I like symmetry, color coordination and balance. They were the personification of a young, successful Sydney. I wanted to take a picture and write a motivational, goal-setting statement under it!

I was interested to hear about how a couple so young had become financially independent. They were yet to have children and I asked them what their goals were now they were wealthy and no longer had to work for a living.

After some thought, Mark simply answered "More."

I then asked him, "Well, then what will you do?"

Their response was not surprising, "We'll travel more, enjoy ourselves, buy a new car more frequently and a house on the harbor would be great."

Penelope loved to shop. I couldn't fault her for that. I then revealed that my husband and I also had sufficient passive income that we could choose to work or not.

I felt the shift in their assessment of me and a new interest in their eyes. I was on their level, and slightly more experienced. After all, I was at the higher end of Generation X!

I then looked at them, smiled and gently said, "Let me ask you a question. You are both of an age that is extraordinarily young to have the wealth you have accumulated. That is not normal. Clearly you have been blessed for a reason. Tell me, what are you doing with it that actually matters?"

They were quite stunned. "We have never thought about it. What do you mean exactly?"

I said, "Everyone has a purpose and everyone is equipped to fulfill that purpose. For example, in Vietnam there is limited nutrition. As a consequence there is a high rate of cleft palate births.

"Through Vietnam Outreach, each month my husband and I pay for a child to have their face repaired. We do it because we can. We've been blessed, so we use that blessing to make a difference in the world. To show them that someone cares."

Mark and Penelope then began to discuss what they might do to make a difference and even create a legacy.

I last heard them talking about creating a college for entrepreneurs so that others could learn how to become wealthy and in turn, make a difference in the world.

We may not all have the great wealth that some people seem to spend with so much ease, but we do have wealth.

The question is "What are we doing that actually matters?"

Be Strategic

I encourage you to run your business world and live your personal life with passion; balanced with purpose and strategy. Don't let past failures stop you from finishing well.

Remember:

- Protect your heart, for out of it does indeed come the issues of life.
- Protect your business, for it is not just about benefitting you and yours.
- There are people waiting for you to bounce back so you can help them get up.
- You don't need another lipstick; you need lips that speak life to others.
- Sharpen your sword, Princess.
- Practice your skills and become stronger.
- There are battles to be fought and won.
- You are called to make a difference in your world.
- You are a Warrior Princess for a purpose.

SERVICES AVAILABLE

How may I serve you further?

How may I help your clients?

- Conference speaking & Seminars
- Consulting
- Coaching
- Warrior Princess Development

Event Planners/Speaker Seekers:

- Do you represent a group such as a Financial Institution?
- Investment Group?
- Business Network?
- MLM?
- Women's group?
- Church or Religious Organization?
- Christian Business Association?
- Singles group?
- Other – Try me!

Allow me to tailor the Dangerous Wealth message just for your people. They will love you for it!

Talk soon!

Trish

Epilogue:

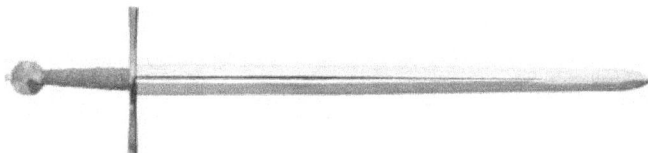

This is the point where you would expect me to say that I now have a perfect life. I triumphed over tragedy. I turned lemons into lemonade. I now live a charmed life and you can too if you follow what I say...

The truth is that as life goes on, fresh challenges regularly present themselves!

The temptation to give up, hide away and live a "safe" life visits me from time to time but like most temptations, it is an illusion. No life is truly safe or problem free.

Success takes courage. Risks are necessary. Publishing this book and exposing my life was scary. Yet by stepping out, I make a difference in people's lives. That in turn, strengthens and fulfills me.

Once I drove myself to succeed unaware of my blind spots. Like Icarus of Greek mythology I flew too close to the sun.

The good news is that now I can identify with the ancient Hebrew Joseph who had been misunderstood, imprisoned but was later trusted with the wealth of Egypt.

In the past, I gave great motivational, success talks. Then, shortly after returning from prison, I received an invitation to speak at a business breakfast.

I felt I needed to let the speaker seeker know how I had "blown it" and give him the opportunity to withdraw the invitation.

To my surprise, his response was, "Now I want you to speak even more. Your story is real and you have keys that will greatly benefit our businesses."

My prison experience will be the subject of a very different, very personal book in diary form taken from letters I sent to my husband. He then emailed edited versions to our friends and family. The book will include what could not be said due to mail being vetted by prison officials.

To bring perspective, I will be adding hindsight commentary. My emails documented my rollercoaster ride from the horrors of the lock-up to high security on to a half-way house and a bounce back to maximum security.

I encountered many colorful characters, some tragic, some inspiring. By the time I was discharged, our email list had grown from a handful to over 100. It seems my stories of tragedy and hope were touching friends as well as strangers.

The core purpose of writing of my journey is to inspire and help people. If you need some inspiration then register on my website: www.dangerouswealthsecrets.com, where you can stay informed regarding the release date for this new book.

I make a difference in the world and so do you.

The Final Princess Warrior Challenge...

 ⸙ Do you believe your life has a purpose?

 ⸙ Do you believe your talent has a purpose?

 ⸙ What are you currently doing that improves the life of anyone beyond yourself and your family?

 ⸙ Are you convinced you are of infinite value?

 ⸙ Do you realize that every other human being around you is of infinite value with massive potential?

 ⸙ Are you prepared to unlock the potential in those around you without feeling threatened by it?

 ⸙ What have you done that will leave an impact on this world when you are gone?

 ⸙ What can you do now that will leave a positive effect on the world after you have left?

 ⸙ What three things will you resolve to do or change after reading this book?

 ⸙ Who else will benefit from reading this book?

 ⸙ Name five women you would like to bless with this book. Now, what are you going to do that will actually matter?

Recommended Resources:

(Contact details are correct as at time of writing)

Trish Jenkins – Keynote Speaking

See Services on Page 198

www.speakertrishjenkins.com   and   www.trishjenkins.com.au

Christian Ministry website: www.trishjenkinsfaith.com

Phoenix Global – Private and Corporate Investigation Bullet Proof Your Business

Mick Featherstone – CEO, Chief Investigator and Author

The Bullet Proof Your Business Program will provide business owners with checklists, templates, procedures and ongoing advice to protect their business from fraud.

Life After Liquidation

Mark Kenway - CEO and author www.lifeafterliquidation.com

For Security - Personal and Workplace: Life-Force One International

Earl Morris - CEO, Senior Threat Management Advisor, Trainer and Speaker www.lifeforceoneinternational.com

For Intercession: Business Blessings

Wesley Leake - CEO www.businessblessings.com.au

Bibliography

Conwell, Russell H. "Acres of Diamonds." Philadelphia: John Y. Huber Company 1890

Dayton, Howard "Your Money Counts." Illinois: Tyndale House Publishers Inc. 1996

Featherstone, Michael. "Bullet Proof your Business" Melbourne: Wilkinson Publishing, 2006

Galbraith, John Kenneth. "The Age of Uncertainty" Boston: Houghton Mifflin Company 1977

Gerber, Michael "The E-Myth Revisited." New York: HarperCollins Publishers Inc. 1995

Hillman, Os. "The Upside of Adversity" Ventura: Regal Books, 2006

Jakobi, Hans. "Due Diligence Made Simple" Portland: Wealth Dynamics International 2001

Maxwell, John C. "Failing Forward Turning Mistakes into Stepping Stones for Success." Nashville: Thomas Nelson, Inc. 2000

Swierczynski, Duane. "The Complete Idiot's Guide to Frauds, Scams and Cons" New York: Penguin Group 2003

Website URLs accurate at time of publication:

www.speakertrishjenkins.com

www.youtube.com/trishjenkins

www.trishjenkinsfaith.com

www.bizactions.com

www.businessblessings.com.au

www.fakechecks.org

www.fraudaid.com

www.peaseinternational.com (Body Language)

www.straightshooter.net
www.sec.gov/investor/pubs/avoidfraud.htm

www.ingramcontent.com/pod-product-compliance
Lightning Source LLC
LaVergne TN
LVHW051051080426
835508LV00019B/1819